FAITH
Without a
DATE

Billy Ray Wheelock

NEWMAN SPRINGS PUBLISHING
320 Broad Street
Red Bank, NJ 07701

First originally published by Newman Springs Publishing 2018

ISBN 978-1-64096-600-0 (Paperback)
ISBN 978-1-64096-611-6 (Hardcover)
ISBN 978-1-64096-601-7 (Digital)

Printed in the United States of America

First of all I dedicate this Book to the real Author, GOD Almighty! For surely every word every event leading up to the manifestation of this Book as well as my Life was ordained and inspired by God. From Him I now turn to the one person that stood firmly by my side every moment of my twenty-one year journey. My heart and soul, my rock, my hero. Yes, my Mother Ms. Rosa Nell Williams. God couldn't have blessed me with a better mother. It would most likely take me another lifetime to replace the pain she had to endure during my absence. But from this day forward I shall supply her with nothing but the purest of my Love. Also I must give my Wife her just due for telling me that I should write this Book but not for self-profit. But for those who may be in need of faith as well as guidance. Last but so far from least, I dedicate this Book to all of my Brother's and Sister's that are still fighting for their right to be free. Please let me be your living testimony as proof that nothing is impossible. So no matter how dim life appears to be, the impossible is always possible with faith.

Contents

CHAPTER 1

The Guilty Verdict

As I sit here in this holding cell totally in shock, my mind is trying its best to make some kind of sense out of all of this while racing in every direction without a finish line in sight! I just sit here wondering, *How in the hell did these people give me life?*

My mind wanders back to the day, all of this took place the day my life changed forever. It was a bright sunny Thursday on May 7, 1992. I had just left the cleaners headed home, as I turned off of Adams street, on to 24 street. I was stopped by the sight of flashing lights. I was then approached by two undercover cops. One I quickly recognized as being Reebok which was the nickname he earned from the streets because of his ability to run down the fastest of criminals. The first thing that came out of his mouth was, "We got you now." Then he went on to say, "You are under arrest for a drug sale! Yeah boy. By the time you get out of this, I will be retired," Reebok said with a sinister smile. Yet who would have known that he would be retired by *suicide*.

As I was being handcuffed, I noticed two young ladies sitting at the 24 street park. They were two sisters I knew. I'm sure they had witnessed this whole ordeal. Yet not in a million years would I have thought they would be the last two individuals in my hometown I would see as a free man, for the next twenty-one years!

I was then taken to our local police station and booked. A few days later, I was transferred to a Federal holding center thirty-five miles away. The unit I was placed in was called the "Glass House." Still not knowing the full extent of my situation and being in unfamiliar surroundings, I simply went into self-preservation mode. Showing no fears as I entered the Glass House. Right away, I knew why they called this place the Glass House. Because the whole unit was totally visible, you could see everything through the glass. As I was headed to my cell, it was like every eye was on me. I could recall seeing something very strange through my peripheral vision as I passed by this opened cell. But I dared to look any closer.

When I got to my assigned cell, I could tell that there was another person staying there, even though he wasn't present. As I went to make up my bed, I heard someone entering the cell. It was a guy they called Smooth. He was cool and made me feel very welcome. So we sat and talked for a long time. He told me why he was there, and I told him the same, until we heard chow time. He quickly jumped up and told me to come on. Man, he was running like it was the last supper. Of course, I was wondering why the rush. I quickly was given the answer to that question once I got down there. To make a long story short, if you're not right there when they are serving, you will miss out completely.

Man, it was all type of people in the Glass House. I mean from dope fiends, to robbers, to murderers, to thieves, to drug dealer, and etc. And they all came out during chow time. Of course, you had the new dope fiends that slept for the first three days straight before resurfacing with an unbelievable appetite.

I really didn't have an appetite, so I gave my tray to my celly (cellmate), Smooth, who gladly accepted. As I was going back to my cell, I passed another opened cell and again through my peripheral vision, I saw that same strange thing happening. For the life of me, I couldn't figure out what I thought I had seen passing those two opened cells. Hey, what I thought I saw was someone over the toilet throwing up or something. I decided to see if my celly (cellmate) had ever noticed this as well, so I planned on asking him when time permitted me to do so. I was quickly brought back to reality by a thunderous sound of commotion. When I looked out my cell to see what was going down, the commotion had stopped. Moments later, my celly (cellmate) entered the cell and told me that there was a fight between two dope fiends over a tray of food. He said the newly arriving dope fiend was late getting down to chow call and missed his tray, so he swung on this other dope fiend that's been in here for months that had two trays and got his whole butt tore out the frame. We laughed and kept on talking.

My celly (cellmate) needed to use the toilet, so I stepped out the cell. And that's when I remembered the question I wanted to ask him, but now I had to wait. So I stood outside of the cell just observing my surrounding. I saw guys working out, guys playing cards, and guys watching TV. Many others were just hanging out talking. Once my celly was done, and the room aired out, I walked back in. I quickly asked him that question I've been wanting to ask him. He started to laugh and told me what I was seeing passing those opened cells was guys talking to their shitter-critter through the toilet.

I was thrown for a loop and just as confused. So I asked him what did he mean and what in the hell was a shittercritter (a nickname given to the women inmates based upon the method of communication)? He explained everything to me. And to make it short and understand-able, right below our unit is the women unit, and if you pump out the water in your toilet with your pillow and they do the same, then both of you will have a direct line of communication to one another. Of course, I was very intrigued with this news, and I quickly asked him does he have one, but before I could get an answer, I heard a loud banging noise coming from our toilet. And he then smiled and said, "Our phone is ringing." As he headed to the toi-let with pillow in hand and proceeded to pump the water out, I was looking at him with pure amazement. Once all the water was out, he got a towel and some disinfectant and sprayed the toilet down really good.

As he was doing this, I heard a girl's voice as clear as day saying, "Honey, are you there?"

And he replied, "Yes, baby, let me finish cleaning the toilet." Again he smiled at me and said, "This is my shitter-critter, and her name is Tina." They talked for hours.

I quickly adapted to my new surroundings and the daily routines of the unit as I was waiting for my arrangement and the full extension of my charge, which came days later. I had been charged with the delivery of one ounce of crack cocaine. At first, I wasn't sure how this happened. Then I recalled selling my little cousin that ounce, which I automatically knew then he had sold it to an undercover agent without knowing. I tried to tell him about dealing with soldiers, who to me *all* looked like the law. Once I thought about this, I knew they really had nothing on me, at least that's what I assumed.

Days became weeks, and weeks became months, and guys came and went just as fast. Daily fighting was normal in the Glass House and drug usage was just the same.

Gambling was the best pastime because those who could get money was allowed to have cash. Of course, the have-nots sought prey to the weak, making extortion very common.

Months later, I received a letter from my court-appointed lawyer stating that I had been offered a plea deal of zero to twenty years. At that moment, all I saw was the possibility of receiving the twenty. And I was already told that in the Feds, you have to do eighty-five percent of your sentence, and that meant if I did happen to get the twenty years, I would have to do almost eighteen years. Listen, I heard about guys that had committed murder that received a lesser plea deal. I just couldn't take that type of chance.

Here I am, a nonviolent criminal, facing a punishment fit for some kind of drug kingpin or murderer. When I refused to accept their deal, they informed me that they would be forming a four-count conspiracy against me and seeking a life sentence. As I was reading this, I thought that there was no way I could receive such a harsh sentence. I simply took it as being a Fed scare tactic.

Breaking news interrupted our daily TV program, and it stated that the Texas serial killer had been captured, and he was being held for expedition back to Texas, by another state. I could feel the silent sigh of relief by everyone watching because it was said that he had killed someone here in this town, and that fear filled the hearts of many.

So many thoughts were constantly invading my mind. The thought of the possibility of me receiving that life sentence haunted me on a daily basis. I tried my best to hide that fear, but so often that fear got the best of me. All I could think about was the effect this would have on my kids and family members. I've been the heart and soul for so many, for so long. Without me, what would become of those whom I love? That was a question I had no answer to. With overwhelming amounts of pressure on my mind and heart, I too found refuge in the company of my own shittercritter. She had just moved in with Tina, my celly's girl. At first, I wasn't interested in talking to anyone, especially through a toilet.

But with the way my life was going, I needed someone to talk to whenever I needed to. It was hard to do that over the phone, plus those calls cost money. So having my own shittercritter really helped me during those most difficult times.

Just another day in the Glass House and to my surprise, no fighting had erupted. So it was a peaceful day so far. My mind was on my little girl that was just born a few months ago. The thought of me missing her first steps as well as her first words caused my heart to get heavy. I found myself constantly asking, "God, why me? What have I done so wrong to receive this kind of punishment?" Lost in my own sorrow, I heard my name being called. And then I felt someone grabbing my shoulder. It was my celly (cellmate) making sure I heard my name being called for visit. So I jumped up and headed to the cell to put on a fresh orange jumpsuit I had laid neatly under my thin mattress. As I was getting ready, I was wondering who this could be because I wasn't expecting a visit from anyone.

The first person I saw was my little girl, her mother was holding her up to the window, and she was hopping up and down laughing. The sight of her caused my eyes to get heavy, but I refused to let a tear fall. Not because I didn't want to. I just couldn't show that degree of emotions around so many other eyes that were watching my every move. Yet had I known this would be the last time I would see my little angel for the next twenty-one years, I would have gladly, as well as proudly, shed those tears. It wasn't a long visit, but it was a good one. My eyes must have known this would be the last time they would physically look upon the beauty of my little girl because they never looked away from her. Her mother tried her best to get their attention but that was truly a lost cause.

Today was a good day, and I held on to that day for too many years to count. I was quickly snapped back into reality when this chair flew by my head. There went this peaceful day, I said while moving out of the way of this ongoing fight between a big white boy and this very slim black guy. Though the white boy had the size advantage, the slim black guy had the hands, and with every connection came a cutting blow and down went Goliath.

CHAPTER 2

The Arrival of the Texas Serial Killer

It was five of us, sitting at the Poker table with a sixth seat open, and Texas Holden was the game. At the moment, I happen to be winning, with Asian Mike running a close second. We've been playing for hours, only taking a break during chow time. It was close to 6:00 p.m. on this particular day when the front sliding door to the Glass House entrance opened. Normally, the noise would have kept us from knowing someone was about to enter the Glass House. But for some strange reason, on this day all noises ceased you could actually hear a pin drop. This automatically caught all of our attention, and when we turned to see what was going on, there stood this six foot four frame of a man that weighed around 295 pounds with a stare that seemed to penetrate through whatever or whomever it looked upon. Fearlessly he walked to his assigned cell. There wasn't a single doubt in anyone's mind when it came to who this strange man was. The whispers of the Texas serial killer echoed throughout the Glass House.

Yet moments later, all actions resumed as if nothing had happened. An hour later to our surprised, the Texas serial killer approached the poker game and asked if he could join us. And being that there was a vacant sixth seat, we said yes, if he had the cash. He reached in his orange jumpsuit and pulled out a wad of money. And one of the players smiled and said, "Let the gambling begin."

It was midnight before the game ended. And I can tell you this much, there were only two winners, and I was one of them. The other winner was Asian Mike. The serial killer lost big time, but he never lost his sense of humor. I guess because in his other pocket was another wad of money he happily displayed as he was leaving the table. At the same time, he stated, "Let's see if you all can win this wad tomorrow."

A couple of days had passed before we had enough players to resume our poker game. And when we finally had enough players, we decided to start after last chow. Today I talked to my mother, and I was still laughing at the conversation we had. She was threatening to call down here because she did *not* like the idea of the Texas serial killer being placed in my unit. I tried to tell her not to worry, but you know how mothers are. They are very protective of their child no matter how old or how big they may be. Trying to be humorous, I sarcastically asked my mother if she would like to talk to the serial killer, and she screamed out "Hell no, and your butt better stay your distance as well." I couldn't stop laughing, but she found nothing funny about it.

Well, last chow was a great disappointment as always. Peanut butter sandwiches with a bag of chips. But the good news is that today was our commissary day, so for those who could afford to shop did just that. The poker table was full, and the gambling was good.

To everyone's surprise, the Texas serial killer had a fan. Some new guy that must have come in the unit unnoticed. We quickly recognized his homosexual tendency. He was all over the serial killer, waiting on him hand and feet. The serial killer went as far as saying, "Punk luck is good luck." But that luck didn't last long. The serial killer was the first player to tap out and leave the game. But the million-dollar question was, was it because of losing or was his mind on more than the game?

It was getting close to lock up time, and as I was going to my cell, I noticed the homosexual going inside of the Texas serial killer's cell. I automatically knew what was going down. The homosexual wanted to spend the night with the Texas serial killer, so they did the Ole Switcheroo with the serial killer's cellmate. You see, when the officers count us at night, they only count bodies, they never ask our names. So getting away with the switch was very easy.

The next morning, everyone was waiting to see what will happen next. To everyone's surprise, it was a quiet morning, and when the homosexual finally came out of the serial killer's cell, you could tell something was different about him by the way he was walking. It was still very early, so I decided to go back to sleep. An hour later, I was awaken by keys rattling and doors being locked. My cellmate had witness what had went down and was telling me everything. He told me that moments ago, the homosexual checked in and told the officer that the Texas serial killer had forced him into his cell last night and raped him. Of course, we all knew that was a lie. At the same time, what better way to get out of his present state of condition than to claim being raped by someone that really shouldn't have been placed in population from the start. The homosexual saw the opportunity and used it to his advantage. And the Texas serial killer was placed in segregation where he remained for the duration of his stay. Months later, this well-known Texas serial killer was found guilty and given the death penalty.

CHAPTER 3

When the Justice System Looks One Way

I finally got my court date. So I was trying to help my court-appointed lawyer prepare for the trial, but he was still trying to convince me to take the plea deal. But I still refused to do so and to my surprise, he really got upset because of that. I should have known I wouldn't have his sincere effort in defending me during trial. But what could I do? True to their every word, they had successfully formed a conspiracy against me, and they also filed for the life sentence. This is just what happens "When the justice system looks one way." I was doing my best to help myself, so lately I've been focusing my time on my case and doing a lot of researching in my cell.

On February 28, 1993, I can remember this like it was yesterday. I was in my cell looking over my paperwork when I heard the loudest roar ever. I mean it was like the Super Bowl was playing. I heard screams of cheering and everything. When I went to see what was happening, I saw guys standing up on tables and chairs, screaming out things like "Shoot them, kill them." Yeah. The TV was showing a raid on this cult compound, and the agents were getting more than they might have been counting on. And this was most entertaining for the held Federal detainees who were extremely delighted with the outcome of this raid. And please, do not get it misconstrued. For these Federal detainees were cheering for the cult people, not for the Federal agents. Of course, this is to be expected when the justice system looks one way.

I have to admit, even though I was facing a life sentence, and the justice system was trying its best to crucify me, I refused to join the cheering. At the same time, I could truly understand the reasons behind their cheer. A 100-to-1 ratio was the fuel for those cheers. You see, if you had one gram of crack cocaine, they charged you for having one hundred grams. Yet if you had one gram of powder cocaine, they charged you just for that one gram. On the most part, all minority groups are the ones that are punished with that 100-to-1 ratio, and the majority of that group happens to be African Americans. Powder cocaine is used and sold mostly by white Americans, and they are only punished by what they actually sold or whatever they are caught in possession of.

Yet what if the justice system decided to make powder cocaine a 100-to-1 ratio? What would white America have to say when their sons and daughters are facing these type of harsh sentencing? The death of this prominent basketball star gave way to a war on a drug that had nothing to do with his death, matter of fact. Powder cocaine should have been the drug of choice held accountable. No one should be held accountable for more than what the crime consist of. If you stole one bike, you shouldn't be charged for stealing one hundred. If you wrote one hot check you should not be charged with writing a hundred.

No charge should be multiplied. Yet today I face a life sentence, not because I had or sold a lot of drugs, not because I committed a violent crime, no, it was *only* because of a law that was given the right to multiply my drug amount by one hundred. This is truly a prime example of when a justice system looks one way.

I was on my way to make my first court appearance. It was time to pick our jury. While waiting in this holding cell at the courthouse, there came three guys. I could tell something different about them once they started to talk to one another. I automatically knew a couple of them where from another country by their accent. The next thing that took place let me know just how different these people were. This black guy that spoke to me had a very strong African accent, to such a degree that I barely understood what he was asking me. "My friend," he proceeded to say, "do you have a paper and pencil?" My reply was yes, and as I handed him those two items, he went on to say, "My friend, for you giving me these two things, I shall give you a paper and pencil factory. *Yes*, these are the things my leader was trying to get out to the world. The Seven Seals is the key that shall open all gates to heaven, yes, the Seven Seals." Man. I was looking at this person like he was crazy, so he quickly stopped talking to me and started talking to his people. I knew just who they were after that short conversation. I had seen on the news where some of the compound people got out before the rest were casualties of that horrific fire. Very strange people they were and still lost in the beliefs of their late cult leader. Yet they too fell prey to when the justice system looks one way.

CHAPTER 4

My Life Taken

The jury had been chosen and a few days later, the trial began. Right from the start, my court-appointed lawyer asked the judge to be dismissed from my case, sighting failure to communicate with one another. Of course, the judge denied his request leaving me with a lawyer that had no interest in representing me. I was doomed from the start. My lawyer did just enough to not be disbarred. I was found guilty on every charge, and all I felt was my life taken.

A few weeks later during sentencing, I was given a twenty-year sentence for count three of the conspiracy, and a twenty-four-year sentence for count two of the conspiracy, and then they enhanced the two counts (by calling them my prior convictions) and gave me a mandatory life sentence, all to be run concurrently. All of this was done because I wouldn't accept their plea deal nor would I give them information on other individuals. They actually made up a conspiracy while I was sitting in jail. Total manipulation at its best. As I sit here in this holding cell, totally in shock, my mind trying its best to make some kind of sense out of all of this while running in every direction, without a finish line in sight. I just sit here wondering, *How in the hell did these people give me life?*

On my way back to the Glass House, all hopes, all dreams had perish. My life had been taken, my heart had been ripped apart, and all that remained was an empty shell. Shaking my head in total disbelief, my body totally numbed, my mind totally lost. I had no sense of direction, and I felt no purpose. I was walking in darkness, totally blind. My mind forgot how to guide me, and I found it hard to breathe. How or when I got back to the Glass House, I can't begin to tell you. How I got to the phone is an even bigger mystery. My mother's voice brought me back from that very dark place, and I lost all sense of control, and I screamed out, "Oh, Mama, they gave me *life*. Mama, Mama, what am I to do? Oh god, Mama, why has my life been taken?" I was crying like a newborn baby, tears running wildly. At that moment, I didn't care about who was watching me. I wasn't concern about hiding my emotions.

Then all a sudden, it was like my mother's voice came through the phone and slapped me not once, not twice, but three times or more with a tone I had *never* heard before. She screamed out, "You shut that mess up, and I mean right now. I don't care what those people told you, you just believe in the *Lord*. Boy, you hold your head up and don't you *ever* break down like this again." Immediately my whole mind, body, and soul transformed into "faith without a date."

CHAPTER 5

Preparing for This Unknown Journey

It's been a week now, and all of my legal matters have been completed. My lawyer had the nerve to tell me that he would be filing my appeal, and I quickly informed him that I would be seeking another lawyer for my appeal process. Since that phone conversation with my mother, my faith level had been indescribable. My spirit had also become unshakable. I've pretty much have said all my goodbyes, and now I'm only preparing for this unknown journey. I've been told that I should be catching the chain (meaning leaving here) in the early morning hours, when my time comes. I've accepted the facts of my situation, but *never* will I accept the sentence. And I will fight this sentence until freedom comes. And I shall do this one day at a time.

I'm hoping they will be transferring me somewhere close to home, but at the moment, I have no clue where I will be placed. Doing federal time is so different from doing state time. The biggest difference is the meaning of a life sentence. In state prison, you can come up for parole on a life sentence after serving a good amount of time. But in the federal prison system, life means life, there's no paroling out. Yes. Life in the federal system means, "You have to die in order to be set free." But I know that will not be the way I shall be leaving here. Because I have faith even though I have no date.

With such a harsh sentence, I decided to cut all ties with the women in my life because even though I know one day I will be freed, I have no right to ask any woman to wait on that day. I know some will claim to be strong enough to handle the waiting, but I know better than that. Plus I wasn't the kind of man that deserves that degree of commitment. Remember, I did say I decided to cut all ties with the *women* in my life, so it's not like I was Mr. Faithful out there. So I didn't expect faithfulness in return. My only wish is that my kids' mothers will keep me close to my kids' hearts. It's really been hard for me to explain my situation to them. All they want to know is when I'm coming home.

Surely it's times like these that make you regret every bad decision you made. I can tell you now, nothing is worth losing time with your kids and family members. But sometimes, it takes losing it all to be able to truly embrace just how important it is to do what is right. Yes, my punishment was too the extreme, at the same time, had I not made those choices, I wouldn't have been put in the position to receive such a harsh sentence. So it's really simple. Just don't do the crime, and you won't have to ever worry about doing this type of time.

I can't began to tell anyone all that I was now going through. I've simply isolated myself away from everyone and everything. Though I have the faith, I still question God because for the life of me, I just can't understand *why*.

But I guess sometimes, we just can't see the forest because of the trees, but that doesn't mean it doesn't exist. So even though I was given life, doesn't mean this life sentence will be my final destiny. Yes, it would be much easier to give up and to give in. But then what? I'm not the first one to endure this kind of pain and suffering, and I won't be the last. I realized that I have to have the faith of Job who lost everything: his wife, children, servants, and wealth, yet he *never* lost his faith in God. So while preparing for this unknown journey, I prepared to survive.

It was around 3:00 a.m. early that Thursday morning, June 24, 1993, when I was awakened by the Glass House unit officer, informing me to pack up my legal material only and get ready to be transferred. Of course, this news caught me and my cellmate by surprise, who was also awakened by the arrival of unit officer. At the same time, we both knew this day would come, just didn't expect it to come this soon. Matter of fact, I had a visit planned for this upcoming Saturday. It was my best friend who is in the military. As the unit officer left the cell, I began to gather my paperwork and mentally preparing for this unknown journey.

I had no idea where I was going, and as I was getting my paperwork together, I said a silent prayer asking God to watch over me as I embark upon this unknown journey. Thirty minutes later, the unit officer returned for me. As I was leaving the cell, my cellmate wished me the best, and we said our goodbyes. When I got downstairs to the holding cell, it was eight of us being transferred, yet no one knew their designation. By 7:00 a.m. that morning, we were on our way out.

A few hours later, after picking up other federal inmates from other federal holding centers, we arrived in another federal holding center in Austin, Texas, where we stayed the night. We were all glad that ride was over because it's very uncomfortable chained down the way we were. They had a chain around our waist, with handcuffs through the chain. Our ankles were also chained. You could feel the ankle cuffs cutting through your skin, on your hands, and ankles, making it a very uncomfortable trip. So we were very happy to get those chains off. Not to mention we were told that at this federal holding center, we will be told just where we will be transferring to. This news really had me thinking and hoping.

After being there for a while, we began to go through the administrative admission, this is where they tell us where each of us will be going. When I finally got called in, I was told I was being transferred to the State of Indiana. When I asked why I was being transferred so far from my family, I was told because there was no USP (United State Penitentiary) in the State of Texas. Therefore, being that I was given a life sentence, my custom level was automatically high. Which places me in a USP (United State Penitentiary) Institution. All that was left for me to do is prepare for the unknown.

CHAPTER 6

When It Rains, It Pours

After all I've been through, now this. When it rains, it pours. Again I asked God why me? As I was leaving, I was totally in shock again. All I could think about is *never* being able to see my family. It was like I was sentenced to spend the rest of my life on the moon. Because there was no way my family members could afford to come visit me. I was feeling so down, even more down than before, but this time, I didn't allow this to break me down. I could still hear my mother's voice telling me to stay strong, and I did just that. You would have thought things couldn't have gotten any worse. Well, think again. Because when I got back to the holding cell, there were about ten of us waiting to go back to our cells when this one guy started asking everyone where they are being transferred to.

The first guy said he was being transferred to an FCI (Federal Correctional Institution) in Texas which happens to be a medium institution. The other few guys stated similar institutions. When he finally got to me, I told him Indiana USP, and he went *crazy*. Screaming out things like "Oh My God, no, no, not there. I just left that place, and they were killing each other like mad men." He screamed, "They even tried to make me kill someone, and when I refused to do so, they beat me up bad." He was shaking and about to cry telling us his story. I tried my best to hide my fear. All kinds of thoughts were going through my head. I'm just saying when it rain, it pours. I just wanted him to stop talking. I could see the way this was affecting everyone, and they weren't the one going to such a place.

Finally, he stopped talking about it, and it was a silence like no other that filled the holding cell. No one said a word, but every so often, I would catch one of them looking at me with this look that said, "I'm glad I'm not going where he's going." I didn't know what to think, but I did know this much, I wasn't going to let anything happen to me. So if madmen were their theme, then a madman I will become.

The next morning, we were on our way to the main federal holding center in Oklahoma, which happened to be over an eight-hour bus ride. Man that was the most uncomfortable ride ever. The chains where eating my wrists and ankles up. Yet all I could think about was my kids and family members. It was so much on my heart, and I didn't know what would come to be. Not knowing caused me unbelievable pain and suffering. But I had to stay strong and focus because I had people depending on me to do just that.

Thank God, we had finally made it to Oklahoma. What a painful long ride it was. It was a very long trip for two reasons, one was the chains, and the other was the small sack lunch we were given for that long ride. So everyone was very hungry when we arrived. We all looked forward to a hot meal. It took a couple of hours to get processed in, so again we had to settle for another sack lunch because we were still in the holding cells during the evening meal. It was late when we finally got to our assigned holding unit.

The unit was full of guys from all over the United States. Some were in the TV rooms watching movies, others were outside smoking. Then you had guys playing cards and chess. I noticed these things while headed to my assigned cell. Once I entered the cell, I made up my bed, and I sat down to gather my thoughts. While doing so, this guy came in, and he introduced himself as the person who was also assigned to this cell. I in turn introduced myself. It was a pleasant exchange. He went on to explain to me how things were there. As we were talking, I had been thinking about where I had been designated to and how I would be getting there.

That's when I found out that I would be catching the Blue Bird, which happens to be a Federal airplane. Airplane, I repeated. His response was "Yes, an airplane, how else did you think you would be getting to the State of Indiana?" To be honest, I hadn't thought about it. With everything that's been going on, now I've got to add a first time airplane ride, surely when it rains, it pours. There's two things I'm terrified of. And they are snakes and airplanes. And right about now, I'll take the snake. Like my grandfather used to always say, "If God intended us to fly, we would have all been born with wings."

A couple days had passed when I was again awakened by the unit officer that early morning to pack out. This time, I was very nervous because I was told that I would be catching the Blue Bird from here. Hours later, I was boarding this very cheap and worn airplane, and it looked like there was some duct tape on one of the wings. The sight of that plane brought fear to my heart. And to make matters worse, we were chained up once again. I was so scared, and my body was shaking. All kinds of thoughts were running through my mind. I saw the plane crashing before it took off. God knows had I known my life would be this messed up, I would have never made these types of choices. It seemed like the punishments never stop coming. But I did know this much, I was not going to sit by the window.

The Plane was crowded with federal men inmates, as well as with federal women inmates. But what caused me to feel a little comfortable was the behavior of all the Federal agents. They were just laughing and talking like they didn't have a care in the world. At first, I tried to justify their behavior by saying that I'm sure they all have parachutes. Then I thought about all the planes I've heard about crashing, and not once did I hear about somebody escaping by parachute, especially from a plane this big. So that told me that if they're not worried about crashing, why should I?

To my surprise, the flight was very fun and not scary at all. To be honest, I actually enjoyed it. I even had the nerves to look out the window. I thought to myself that flying is really the way to travel, and I was sure I would like to experience flying again, but next time hopefully without the chains.

CHAPTER 7

My First Designation

I'm now on the Federal bus headed to my first designation. All I could think about is what that guy was telling us about this USP in Indiana. It took us an hour before we got there, and as we were approaching the institution, I couldn't see the institution that good because of all the gates and barb wire fences. I will admit that the institution was looking just the way that guy had described it, and that caused me to feel a little sick inside.

Again, I said a silent prayer to God asking him to watch over me.

As I was being escorted off the bus, I noticed that the institution was very old. And when I got inside, that fact was confirmed because it had no AC (air-conditioning). Man, the living conditions were bad there. Finally, I was assigned to my unit, which I soon found out that it was the worse unit there. D Unit aka the Dog House. When I entered that unit, it was like entering into another part of the world. The lights were dim, and the cigarette smoke formed a cloud you could barely see through. It was like walking through a western saloon. All I could say was, that guy wasn't lying. One guy tried to ask me a question, and before I knew it, I snapped on him in a very mean way. I didn't mean to, but I was really on guard.

I walked into the unit officer's office and got the number of my assigned cell. So with bed roll in hand, I headed to my cell. Once I got there, I started to make my bunk, and once I was finished, I sat down to gather my thoughts. I could tell that there was another inmate assigned to this cell, so I just waited for him to join me. About an hour later, this bald-headed black guy entered the cell. Being the man I am I spoke to him, but I got no response. I was already on guard and even though he made me feel very uncomfortable by not responding. I refused to say another word to him. So that was that, we never said a word to one another. Like I said, there was no air-conditioning, and it was dead in the middle of summer time when I arrived. The heat was unbearable during the day and night, to such a degree that with the only money I had, I bought a fan, and I mean I did this the next day. That's how hot it was. When daytime came, the unit that looked so damn gloomy came to life, and it wasn't nearly as bad during the daytime. I found out that there was even a guy from Texas in the unit, he was from Austin, Texas, only seventy-two miles from my hometown. And being that we were from the same state, we automatically connected. They call him Tex. Anyway, I and Tex hit it off great. During lunch time, he introduced me to four more of our homeboys. That gave us a total of six guys from Texas out of 1,600 inmates.

Also that next day, I called my mother to let her know where I had been transferred, of course the distance that separated us made her very unhappy, but I told her I would be okay. I could tell she was still worried, so I tried to make her feel even more relaxed about my situation, by telling her that I did have homeboys down here with me. Of course I didn't tell her how many of us were there because she would have started back worrying.

I've been here over a week now and to my surprise, nothing so dramatic has happened, so I'm beginning to think that the guy that told us all these terrible things wasn't being all that accurate. At the same time, I was in a very bad unit, and I was told by my homeboys that I should try to get out of there. I was already thinking about making that move, more so because I and my cellmate still haven't spoken one word to one another. I really didn't know what his problem could be, because I have tried to start several conversations, but he refuse to talk. But what really got me to move was what happened the next night. It was another very hot night, even with the fan blowing directly on me I was still very hot. To be honest, the fan was only blowing hot air, but hot air was better than no air. On this hot night, the fan was the only thing allowing me to sleep. Yet while I was in a very deep sleep, I felt my body feeling like it was overheating. Moments earlier, I thought I heard a loud clicking sound. All of a sudden, I felt sweat running across my face. This caused my eyes to finally open. What I noticed next made my blood rush to my head. My fan had been moved, and it was now pointing down on my cellmate. Man, I almost broke my fan turning it back up to me at the same time. I stared down at my cellmate with a look that could have killed.

My first thought was to jump down off the top bunk and start hitting him dead in his face. It took everything inside of me not to do just that. The nerve of this guy to have the audacity to touch my fan, and he hasn't said two words to me. My blood was boiling, and I kept staring down at him hoping he would try touching my fan again. But not only did he not try that again, he didn't move an inch, it's like he knew his life was in jeopardy. Finally, after a couple of hours I drifted back to sleep. When I finally woke up, he was up and gone. Hours later, I was on my way to not only to a better cell, but also a better unit.

CHAPTER 8

The Adjustment

Getting adjusted to my new surrounding took some time. Like I said, all of this was so new to me, and being so far away from home didn't make the adjustment any better. This was a very old institution. And being that the winter months got very bad up here, it was built where you never had to leave the inside of the building to get to anywhere. Except when you wanted to go outside. At the same time, everything you may have wanted to do outside you could also do on the inside. They had an inside gym with weights to lift and a basketball court to play basketball or handball. The bad thing about going to the gym, it was one way in and out, plus you were locked inside of there, and most of the time unsupervised. This made the gym area a very unsafe place to be especially if a riot was to take place. There was also a hobby craft area located upstairs of the gym.

A recreational center was located in the middle of the institution. The bad thing about it was that you had to go up four tiers of stairs with every tier having a blind spot. It was designed like a hall with stairs and no cameras. So it was also a very dangerous place to go. I had heard that there had been lots of assaults that have occurred in that area, some were even fatal. There were several pool tables up there, ping-pong tables, and the band rooms were also located in that area. Plus it was an area up there where they held prison concerts, with a leisure area where cards or other tabletop games could be played.

Right after the center was the chapel and then the dining hall (lunch room). The educational and legal department alone with library area was located across from the chapel. On that same side, you had the main staff area which was not accessible to inmates. On that same side, you had the main staff area which was not accessible to inmates mainly because the warden office was located in that area, with all other main staff members' offices. Then came the lieutenant's office and then the institutional hospital. Right across from the lieutenants office was a walk area that led you directly to the Federal Prison Industry also known as Unicor and FPI, which is a wholly-owned United States government corporation created in 1934 that uses penal labor from the Federal Bureau of Prisons to produce goods and services. FPI is restricted to selling its products and services to federal government agencies. Prisoners make between twenty-three cent and SI point fifteen per hour. Unicor has 109 factories in federal prisons, producing about 175 different types of products and services. At this Unicor, their specialty is mailbags and textile. The units were located between and before those areas.

The recreational outside area's main attraction was the gun tower which looked like it was a half of a football field up in the air which sat in the middle of the yard. With two armed Federal officers ready to fire upon anyone who is attempting to commit a violent assault against a staff member or an inmate. You will only find this kind of tower in a USP (United States penitentiary) which means a prison for people who are convicted of serious crimes. It was a very huge yard. There were two baseball fields, two basketball courts, both located on opposite sides of the yard, with two tennis courts, and four handball courts right next to each other. Then you had two large areas with weights and an area with boxing bags. There was even a large Putt-Putt golf course. To be honest, it looked more like a country club resort out there. To top that, the inmates were allowed to wear street warm-ups of all colors. So everyone looked like regular people.

I had heard that I missed being able to order fast food by a year. They used to be able to order fried chicken or pizza on the weekend. Being in the Federal system truly had its French benefits at that time. I was amazed by all of this. Again, I was beginning to think what I was told by that guy about this place wasn't all that true. Until I began to notice the strong presence of gang activity. Just to name a few, you had the Crips and Bloods, then there was the Vice Lords, Gangster Disciples, Latin Kings, Italian Mafia, Aryan Brotherhood, the Mexican Gangs consisted of the following gangs: Pizzas, Tango Blast, and Border Brothers. It was very important that the Mexican Gangs' members be thoroughly interviewed before entering into population. Because if they were members of any of the rival gangs, their life would be at danger at first sight.

Then came the Cars (it's a group of inmates from the same state joining forces together) you had the D.C. Car from Washington, D.C. which also included Maryland inmates as part of the D.C. Car. I quickly learned that the D.C. Car was truly a force to be reckoned with throughout the Federal system. Mainly because of the large amount of them in the system. Then there was the Florida Car, St. Louis Car, New York Car, Michigan Car, Georgia Car, and the Alabama Car. Of course, there were other cars, but their numbers weren't big enough to make a difference.

Though I wouldn't consider the religion groups as gangs or cars, they are just as important to mention because they too represent unity and if pushed the wrong way, they could become just as lethal. Especially the Muslim groups. You had the Christians, Sunnah Muslim, Nation of Islam, and the Moorish Science Temple. Every gang, car and group had their own section in the dining hall. And no one crossed that dining hall section rule.

The smallest incident between any of the above mentioned could turn into a full-fledged riot. Yet the biggest riot that was feared was a racial riot. So everyone did its part to make sure it never got to that point. I have to be honest, everything about this place was so new to me. I didn't know anything about these gangs or these different religion groups. The closest thing I knew about a Muslim was watching the Malcolm X movie.

So adjusting to all of this was an adventure within itself.

I was truly feeling blessed because my new unit which was C unit, was very laid-back. Matter of fact, it was an honor unit. I had a nice cellmate, and we got along good. I also met a guy I called Pops who took me under his wing and taught me how to adjust to my new life in a United State penitentiary. He looked out for me as if I was his own son. He really taught me a lot. I had nothing but love and respect for my Pops. He was a true OG that wore his baseball caps cocked to the side. He demanded respect from not only from every inmate but from the officers as well. He was out of St. Louis and was the leader of the St. Louis Car. I learned that every gang, car, or group had a leader. During the course of the upcoming months, other than a few minor stabbings here and there, it wasn't so bad. Mainly because the incidents were in-house activities meaning, disagreements within said gang, car, or group and not against one another.

It was only six of us from Texas, so we stayed pretty close. T-Boy was also from Austin, Texas, and we hung out a lot together. Because it was safer being with someone when you went out and about. So being that we were homeboys, and he lived across the hall, we always got together. He was in for committing arson, which he said caused injuries to a couple of people. It was a common thing to know why one was doing time. Matter of fact, it was mandatory that you showed your legal paperwork to your homeboys, gang, car, or group because they wanted to make sure of two things, one, you're not a snitch, or two, you're not a child molester. If you're found to be either one of those things, your life would surely be in jeopardy. Because those two things were highly frowned upon within the United State penitentiary.

I was glad to have stood firm when it came to accepting my own faith and keeping all others' information to myself. I come from the old school, if you do the crime, be man enough to do the time. Snitching was *never* an option and never will be one.

CHAPTER 9

A World Away from Home

I and T-Boy were outside chilling, and all I could think about was being a world away from home. He's telling me about a club in Austin, Texas, that he used to go to. And I was telling him that I've been there a few times myself. Of course, we never ran across one another, but it was still cool knowing we had been to the same club. I would have never thought what I was about to find out would actually bring this world I was now living in, right inside my mother's home.

My mother had just sent me some funds, so I put a couple of dollars on the phone to call her and thank her. She was happy to hear from me as always, and of course she was curious to know what I've been doing and whom I've been hanging with. So I told her about my friend T-Boy, being that he's the one I'm with most of the time. Just like my mother, she wanted to know more about him. The main thing she wanted to know was why he was there. My mother is very protective, and she just wanted to make sure I'm not hanging with someone that would get me into trouble. So I told her where he was from and just what he told me he was in here for. I told her that he was from Austin, Texas, and he was in here for arson. He told me that they said he started a fire at this apartment complex, and a couple of people got hurt. I was waiting for her to respond, and it was like she wasn't on the phone so I said, "Mother, are you still there?" What seemed like ten seconds went by before she said hold on.

Sixty seconds later, she returned to the phone and told me to tell her boyfriend John about my friend T-Boy. This was very strange to me, but I simply did what she asked of me. I told him just what I told my mother just moments ago. But when I got to the part where T-Boy said a couple of people got hurt, John, my mother's boyfriend, quickly interrupted me and stated, "No, it wasn't a couple of people that got hurt, my sister-in-law, my niece, and nephew died in that fire, and ninety-five percent of my brother's body was burned, but he lived." I was speechless, and I was in shock. I didn't know what to say.

That's when I heard my mother's voice, and she begged me to stay away from my friend T-Boy. Of course, I said I would because I didn't want to worry her. When I hung up the phone, I was still in shock and confused. First of all, I didn't want to act different toward my friend, at the same time, I didn't want to worry my mother. So after thinking about this all night, I decided to leave well enough alone. When I saw T-Boy, I acted the same way as always, and I never told him about what I had found out. The next time I spoke to my mother, I told her just what she wanted to hear. I told her that I was no longer hanging around T-Boy, so she was happy. Who would have known, even though

I'm a world away from home, this world could still reach into my own mother's home?

I was determined to fight for my freedom. It was truly an uphill battle, but I kept my faith.

Though I knew very little about the law, there was one thing I was certain of, and that was the life sentence I was given wasn't right. So I had to stay focus. You see, the system was designed to bury you even deeper. Its sole purpose was to keep you inside by allowing you to fall prey to either gang-related activities, or the prison traps that awaited that unaware prisoner.

It was so easy to grab a whole to something when you had nothing but a lot of time to do. And most of the time, that something wasn't good for you. The gangs and cars preyed upon that need one had to reach out for that needed something. They used that weakness to lure you all the way in, and once you were in, there was no way out. At least that was the feeling they gave you. Most of the time, they used those new members as puppets.

They made them responsible for holding their knives and other illegal contraband.

Because they knew the penalty of possession of such a weapon or weapons would result in receiving a new federal charge. And that meant more time added on top of the time you were already serving if you were ever caught. Even though I was a world away from home, I refused to fall prey to *any* gang, car, or group. Yes, I was respectful to all gangs, cars, and groups. I was even friends with some of them. But I stood neutral to it all. I had no opinions, nor did I have any say so on how either one of those three entities conducted their everyday way of life. It was simple, I minded my own business. I quickly learned that was truly one of the best ways of staying safe.

CHAPTER 10

What Does the Weather
Have to Do with It?

It was hotter than hot, and some would ask what does the weather have to do with it? Believe it or not, the weather has a lot to do with the everyday way of life here. You see, when it's extremely hot, that's when moods change, and when moods change, that's when problems are created. On this particular day, everywhere you turned there was some kind of disagreement brewing. On this day, it all started from a three on three basketball game outside dead in the middle of this very hot day. On team one, there was a player that was a Crip, and on team two, there was a player that was a Blood. Of course, they happened to be guarding one another, when one good move caused the biggest argument. What started from two became a full-fledged gang riot. Which ended with a standoff in the middle of the dining hall between the two gangs. They actually took over the entire dining hall for a hot second. Yes, they cleared out all staff members and barricaded the door. I was sure it was going to be a massacre. But it ended with a standoff, with neither gang backing down. Of course, it took only a few minutes before reinforcement joined the few staff members to regain control of the situation. Thank God, there was no blood shed on this very hot day. But with temperature raising day by day, who knows what the next very hot day will bring?

On this very hot summer day, the outcome wouldn't be as fortunate. Again, I happen to be sitting down in the dining hall enjoying my favorite meal (fried chicken) when I heard this loud commotion coming from the serving line. The first thing I saw was a guy with a knife in each hand taped to each hand. He swung both knives into the body of this well-known gang leader, killing him instantly. The gang leader's members came to his aid, and they too were stabbed, one nearly to death, but he survived. It was the bloodiest day I had ever witnessed. I was shaking like crazy and totally in shock. This was the first time I had seen such a gruesome act, the first time I witnessed someone being killed. I was haunted by that vision day and night. My appetite was lost in all the madness. It was said that all of this took place because of a three-year grudge held by the assailant.

The whole institution was placed on lockdown until a thorough investigation had been conducted. The lockdown lasted about three whole days. We were all confined to our cell during the investigation. That was the normal protocol after such a horrific event. We were also all interviewed, which was another measure taken after such an event. Of course, everyone's answers were the same, even if you were there, *you saw and heard nothing*. When we finally got off of lockdown, there were lots of grieving. A week later, there was a special memorial held in the chapel for the well-known victim that lost his life during that horrific event.

The summer time produced numerous of stabbings and fights and of course, occasional deaths. Which placed us on lockdown most of the summer. Yes, the weather had a lot to do with it. When winter finally came, tempers where also cooled down, and it wasn't that many disagreements. Yes, there was a fight or two here and there but nothing like the summer time.

In the fall of 1995, we were all excited about the amendments to bring the disparity into balance by upping the crack levels to be equal with the cocaine levels. Because such a change would automatically lower 100s of thousands of our cases, sending us much closer to the door, if not out the door. I was extremely happy, being that my appeal had been denied, after all the praying. The joy of this news was felt nationwide and highly talked about throughout the Federal system. Every inmate just knew it would be approved, well, every inmate but Pops. Pops had been down for a while, and he had really lost faith in the system. So he didn't want me to get my hopes up.

Then came congress challenging the amendments, and it didn't become law. What started out as the best fall of 1995, in the blink of an eye turned into the infamous crack riots that erupted all across the United States almost simultaneously throughout the Bureau of Prisons. It was said that those riots represented a couple of the darkest days in the history of the Bureau of Prisons, yet it got almost no press or media attention nationwide. I'm pretty sure this may be the first time most of you have ever heard of this. Yet it was one of the greatest acts of unity demonstrated between inmates of every nationality or ethnic groups. There was even a nationwide lockdown throughout Bureau of Prisons behind this movement. Yes, I said movement because it's not often you find inmates coming together in such a magnitude. If you're wondering what the weather had to do with this one, that's truly a question I have no answer to.

CHAPTER 11

Just Maybe

I've been here two years now and just maybe, if Bill Clinton is reelected, he just might be willing to give us that much needed relief we've been hearing about from the time he was first elected. That's been the talk coming from all these major prison advocacy groups. Every time I talk to my kids, they always ask me when I'm coming home, and every time, I tell them maybe next year. And to be honest, I always felt like that would be the case. So now I've got my eye on 1996.

I'm missing my kids and family like crazy. It's been two years now, and I haven't seen anyone. But I did hear some good news today. I was told by a staff member that they were building the first United States penitentiary in the State of Texas, and it should be up and running by 1997. That was the best new I've heard in years. So I was determined to make it until that day comes. This really gave me something to look forward to. Just maybe, my luck was about to change.

With every election year comes a resilient amount of hope. Every inmate hopes that just maybe, this will be the year the crack law gets revised. Especially if President Clinton is reelected. We all knew that during a president's first four years, they will only do so much because their number one goal from the start is being reelected from the first day they arrive at the White House. To be honest, it's almost viewed as a failure not to be reelected. So the first four years is pretty much scripted. They tend to play the first four years safe. Every election year, hopes are raised. And every inmate is paying close attention to the poles.

And though we have no voting rights, doesn't mean we have no say so on who's going to be elected because we do. You see, most of us have family members that love and misses us, and they would do whatever it takes to get us home. If that meant going out to vote, then that's what they would do. All we have to do is let them know who is on our side, and they would gladly go vote for that person. Even though President Clinton did very little for us during his first four years, almost every inmate feels that if he's reelected, he would do more for us on his way out. So with that thought going through the minds of so many inmates, President Clinton will surely receive the support of many inmates' family members.

All with the hope of just maybe, this will be our year. The presidential elections went as planned and President Clinton was reelected to another four-year term. This brought joy to almost every inmate, and we were all extremely happy and very excited about the outcome. We just knew the president would come through for us. I was very excited about the possibilities. 1996 was a very exciting and hopeful year. I was finally working in Unicor which allowed me to stay busy and out of the way.

You see, it's very important to utilize your time wisely because it's extremely easy to fall prey to all of those hidden prison traps. For once in a long time, just maybe, things were looking good for me. Then came the unthinkable. You would have thought nothing worse could happen to me. For the life of me, I just couldn't understand why all of this was happening. *God, what have I done so wrong to receive your wrath?* As quickly as that question was asked, the answer was given as a question just as quick. What have you done so right, to avoid the coming of my wrath?

On October 19, 1996, at about 1:30 p.m. I injured my left leg while playing flag football. The injury occurred when I was attempting to block a pass. As I jumped to block the football, I landed in a hole. The impact sent tremendous pain and numbness to my left leg causing me to fall to the ground. I remained on the ground about twenty minutes before medical staff arrived. I was then taken inside the medical center.

Several days later, I saw the doctor where he immediately arranged for emergency surgery. I was transferred to a local hospital outside the institution where I underwent a five-hour surgery, wherein a nerve specialist was called in during the operation, in an effort to save the badly damaged nerve to my lower left leg. Several hours later after the surgery, I awakened to find myself in a half body cast. I was still feeling the effects of the medication that caused me to lose conscience during surgery. So I was in a dazed state when the doctor informed me that they were unable to save the badly damaged nerve. At the moment, I really didn't know what the effect would be from losing this nerve.

Days later, I found out about the permanent damages to my leg. In addition to the very unattractive scars left by the surgery, I was left with permanent foot drop. Which means that I can no longer pat my left foot. And I would have to wear a brace, so I wouldn't be tripping over things as I walked. I was confined to my room for a month or so. I couldn't do much on my own. So guys like my Pops and other friends made sure they were there for me. I quickly learned that when you're doing time, your true friends become like family. Pops made sure I had the things I needed. He took the best care of me. He was truly one of *God's* angels that watched over me. I just prayed that one day I could return such a blessing.

CHAPTER 12

Downtime

With all of this downtime, my mind tend to run in a hundred different directions. Being confined to my cell after my leg surgery is driving me crazy. At the same time, it's dangerous to be out and about, even if it's just to the TV room because even though I'm in a pretty good unit, there's still a strong possibility that a fight or a riot could happen at a drop of a dime. So with a lack of mobility, it's just safer if I stayed in my cell and out of the way. Yet that doesn't stop my mind from wondering so much.

The number one question that constantly invaded my mind is that what-if question. What if I would have done this or what if I wouldn't have done that? All of these what-if questions, then you have to add reality, plus a lot of missing your loved ones, then a life sentence, and now add a permanent handicap, surely that would come to the sum total of an unbelievable misery. The saying "An idle mind is truly the devil's workshop," is very much understandable if you were to ask me right about now.

So with all the downtime, I decided to do some constructive thinking and writing. Though I've never wrote any poetry, I wanted to try my best to turn my idle mind into something working toward God's workshop. So I thought about the genuine expectations of my parents of me, and then I thought about the choices I made, and that of the consequences that came with those choices. Every aspect of what I'm about to write is that of my own life. And I write it as a warning to those who chose to venture down that wrong path. I entitled this: "What Shall I Be."

What Shall I Be

My father wanted me to be a great athlete.
My mother just wanted the simplest things from me.
One love, one wife, a few grandkids she could keep over
the weekend or during the summer months for a week.
But I chose what is known to me
today as the devilish way.
Ten women I craved for each day. While thinking
of many more that may come my way.
Easy money was my chosen path, I could even be
pleasing another and still be getting payments back.
What shall I be, was a silly question to me. For
I had it all through the eyes that I see. "Hey,
there were even guys wanting to be like me."
Then came the reward for being less than what
I shall be. A nine by twelve cell now houses me.
I have only one question to ask. "Where is just
one of those fools who wants to be like me?"

Believe me, there's nothing glamorous about being in such a place. There's no amount of money worth losing your right to be free. And the time you lose you can never get back. Doing time comes with mountains of regrets. I wouldn't wish a day of this experience on anyone. Today I realize that I would rather be free and broke than to ever experience the loss of my freedom. I can't say when my freedom will come, but I can say this much, when that day finally gets here, I will cherish it with my life, and never will I place myself or my family through this again. I constantly ask God why and though I have not heard his answer, I truly believe within time I shall know that of his purpose.

Even though I truly believe that God has my back, with all of this downtime, I just can't stop my wandering mind. It's like my mind has its own hidden war going on, between two wills. The first will destined to survive, by any means necessary. Mainly by using the Adapt and Overcoming method. Meaning whatever may come my way, I shall face it and find a positive resolution. The second will destined to give up and to give in. Yes, its mission is simple, give in to self-destruction. It even gives one a convincing, as well as a compelling, argument to support its decision. By giving its own understanding of the facts—it starts by stating the obvious: "Just look at you, you're serving a life sentence, you're a thousand miles away from your family members, you've lost everything and if that wasn't enough, you're now permanently handicapped."

It goes on to say. I'm telling you, if you were to give up, not only would it be more than expected of you, there

would be so many of your loved ones making compassionate excuses for you for doing so. And let us not forget about
the many others you would be joining, that took their own
lives for matters, way less than that of your own. I have to
admit, that the second will made some very valid points.
Then out of nowhere came these words, they were entitled
"Self-Destruction."

Upon each day, trials or tribulations may come one's
way; without a thought, self-destruction begins to
play, causing one to judge self, in an unjust way!
Where does it say, self-destruction is a better
way? When the greatest gift is the blessing of
life, that's given to us by the Lord Almighty!
The right to live, is *not* one's right to take away. For
in the beginning was the word, which life followed.
So whenever self-destruction begins to play,
just get on your knees and begin to pray!
It's written to forgive those who trespasses against thee, so
how could one not forgive thyself? Upon each day, trials
or tribulations may come one's way; without a thought
self-destruction begins to play, not knowing that the Lord
Almighty protects thee, even from thyself that they seek!

These words were truly heaven-sent, and I want you all
to understand that had I allowed the second will its way, I
would have never gotten to that better and brighter tomorrow. And God constantly reminds me that my life is truly
worth living. Believe me, there're always a million others
doing way worse. You can't go wrong if you always do what

is right, and I'm speaking of that universal right and not of one's personal understanding of the meaning of right. So with all of this downtime, I've decided to fight to live out my dreams.

CHAPTER 13

Homebound

Extreme excitement filled the hearts of every inmate who happened to be from the South because the rumors were true, they had just finished building the first USP (United States penitentiary) in the State of Texas, and they were accepting transfer request from every inmate from that region, especially inmates from Texas. At last I was homebound.

My leg was healing fast, and I was getting around very well, of course that was with the help of a walking cane. I was even able to go back to work at Unicor, light duty of course. My homeboys were all on cloud nine. T-Boy came out of nowhere and picked me up while shouting out, "Homie, we are homebound." We all put in our transfer request and a couple weeks later, we were all approved.

I called home to tell my family all about the good news, and they were all excited about me coming home. They went as far as starting to plan their trips down to visit me. Even though I still carried the huge burden of a life sentence, going home gave me even more faith and determination. We were all told that we should be leaving sometime next month, which happened to be the month of May 1997.

T-Boy was simply overly excited, he vowed to celebrate every single day he was here.

The week before our departure, T-Boy did a little too much celebrating, and he found his way to the institutional detention housing for being in a state of intoxication. This automatically removed T-Boy from the transferring list. Because even though we were going to another USP (United States penitentiary) the first transferees cannot have any recent incident reports on their record. Now T-Boy had to wait.

Even though I was overly thrilled by the fact that I was about to be homebound, it was very sad saying goodbye to all my newfound friends. Because I viewed them all as family, you see—after four long years here, they were all I had, and I loved them all as my brothers. Shaking hands and embracing my brothers for the last time really touched my heart. But we all vowed to stay in touch, so we exchanged mailing info and left it at that.

The eve before my departure, me and my main man T-Boy took our final few laps around the track saying our goodbyes. Of course, I told him how stupid he was for getting drunk the week before we were to leave. At the same time, we both knew he would still be coming to Texas soon. It wasn't like we were saying goodbye for good so that didn't make this moment as bad. I let him know that I would be saving him a job position. We laughed and joked for a while before we embraced and said we will be seeing one another soon. As I walked away from T-Boy, I was just rethinking about the secret I still carried in my heart about him being the guy that was responsible for the deaths of my mother's boyfriend's sister-in-law, his niece, and nephew. With so many thoughts on my mind, only one spoke out the loudest, "I'm homebound."

CHAPTER 14

There's No Place like Home

I'm sitting here in this transferring holding cell feeling like Dorothy of the Wizard of Oz, constantly repeating "There's no place like home, there's no place like home." Even though I will still be a few hundred miles from my hometown, I still feel so blessed. I guess that's because I'll be in Texas and being anywhere in Texas is a million times better than being in the State of Indiana.

I'm just hoping that this time when I fly out of here it will be on a better-looking plane and not on that old ugly Federal plane they call the Blue Bird. After all, it's been four years now, and that plane looked like it was on its last leg way back then. My heart is racing a hundred mile an hour with excitement. And for the first time in my life, I'm looking forward to the plane ride. I can remember the first time being terrified of the fact that it was going to be my first time ever flying.

We are now on the bus headed to the Federal airport. I took one last look at the institution I had spent the last four years in, and my mind raced down memory lane. And I saw the bad moments, as well as every few good moments

I encountered during those four years. As I turned away for the final time, all I could think of was "There's no place like home." Yet I couldn't shake the feeling of sadness for all of those good friends I'm leaving behind. I couldn't stop thinking about their well-being. You see, I was very aware how in a blink of an eye, one could lose their life for no reason at all. In a United States penitentiary, one's odds of survival is a lower percentage than that of being an FCI (Federal Correctional Institution, which is medium security), or a low security, and a camp.

Of course, I was reminded of the new United States penitentiary I was headed to in Texas, at the same time, I knew it would be a year or better before this penitentiary turn into the hell it was built to be. It was no getting around that fact, but at least the first arrivals get the opportunity to set the tone. So by the time the true killers arrive, we will already have established our place within these walls of confinement. With every thought that invaded my mind, I was still reminded "There's no place like home."

We just arrived at the airstrip, and the first thing I spotted was the Blue Bird. Man, you would have thought they would have retired that ugly ole plane. I saw that same piece of duct tape on that same wing. All I could do was shake my head. But for some reason, I still wasn't afraid. I just put in my mind that they must have given this plane a good overhaul. It was a shaky takeoff, but the overall plane ride was great. As the plane flew above the clouds, I thanked God for keeping me safe for those four years. I must have dozed off because I was awoken by the preparing-to-land speech given by the air pilot, informing us that we will be landing in Oklahoma within minutes.

From there, it was a bus ride to Texas, and the sightseeing was unbelievable, especially when we passed through Dallas, which happened to be only a 120 miles from my hometown. Matter of fact, I used to travel back and forward from my hometown to Dallas, so I was very familiar with the town, it brought back a lots of memories. Of course, it had grown a lot in four years, but I still felt a very strong connection. A few hours later on May 13, 1997, we had arrived at the doorsteps of the first United States penitentiary in the State of Texas.

It's resemblance was very different from the United States penitentiary I just left. But what did remain the same was the gun tower that stood in the middle of the complex. This complex was built in a complete circle. And not like the last institution, we had to leave our Units to go where ever. The unit building went as followed: from right to left you had D Building, C Building, and E Building. There were four units in each building which went as followed: E-1 Lower, E-2 Upper, E-3 Lower, E-4 Upper. C-1 Lower. C-2 Upper, C-3 Lower, C-4 Upper. D-1 Lower, D-2 Upper, D-3 Lower, D-4 Upper. There were twelve units in all. Each unit held around 125 inmates.

To the left of D Building there was a large basketball court, and handball court. To the left of that was an inside basketball court and recreational area that had pool tables and etc. Continuing left you had the chapel and then came the educational department, which also had the library and leisure area enclosed. Then came the warden and staff offices. In that same area was the inmate visiting room. From there, you had the institutional hospital and down a long hall was disciplinary housing center, for misbehaved inmates. Continuing to the left was the officers' dining hall and then came the inmates' dining hall. Then there came the inmate commissary store. Then came the vocational department. Then finally came Unicor, and to the left of that was Building E, which completed the full circle. Like I first said, in the center of this was a gun tower, a circled running track, and two baseball fields, which also served as two football fields.

The units had two-men cells, and inside each cell were two bunks designed like a bunk bed, a sink and toilet, and a small desk with a chair hooked to it. The units were built in a circle as well, with cells up and downstairs. A large horse-shoe desk counter stood in the front of each unit, with the officer's office right behind the desk. To the right of that office were four inmate phones, where inmates could make prepaid or collect calls home. Farther right was a table that held two microwaves for inmates to cook in. A little farther around was an ice machine and the unit counselors office.

Then there came the inmates' TV room and then there came the first inmate cell, which continued around to make a full circle. There was also two microwaves stationed to the right of the officer's horseshoe desk. To the left of the officer's office was another inmate TV room. Upstairs there were two more TV rooms located right above the other two TV rooms, there was also a laundry located to the left of the TV that had two washers and two dryers. Every unit was designed the same.

I was then reminded again that one day soon this place will become the hell it was built to be. But for the moment, it was as good as it could get for the first arriving inmates. At a compound that housed 1600 inmates, the thirty-five of us that stood there first, all had a smile on our faces that outshined the summer sun that stood above us. Without one word spoken from any of us, our hearts spoke the same, "There's no place like home."

CHAPTER 15

Who Would Have Known?

Who would have known this United States penitentiary would be this sweet starting off. Yes, we all knew we would be the first ones here, but to be treated like the staff is treating us seems so surreal. We quickly learned the reason behind the way the staff members were treating us. It wasn't so much of them wanting to do so, as it was of them being ordered to do so by the warden himself. His motto was simple, treat the inmates like you want to be treated. He felt that if you gave respect, you would get respect in return. And yes, he demanded the same degree of respect toward his staff members from every inmate.

The warden was a middle-aged black man that was a former star athlete. It was said that he might have even played some pro ball. He was truly an admirable warden that quickly gained the respect of the majority of inmates. But wasn't all that big of a hit with the majority of the staff members. Because most of the staff there was totally against treating us like humans. Most of their frame of thoughts felt that we were all bad people because we were here. Being stereotyped was a norm throughout the justice

69

system, and that remains the case for the majority of prison institutions. Yet who would have known someone of the warden's statue would be standing on our side so firmly, as well as openly.

This institution was everything and more. It was like being at a college campus. And the food was great. Once they served us fried chicken and fried fish during the same meal. Man, that was unheard of. They fed us so good that you never had to go to the institution store for anything. No one would have known this place would be this unbelievable, at the same time we all knew that it wouldn't be lasting forever, but that didn't stop us from enjoying the moment.

Being the first arriving inmates gave us all first dibs on everything, and we took full advantage of that opportunity. My goal was to get the best job position in Unicor that paid the most. This Unicor happened to be a sewing factory that specialized in putting together army fatigues. With the Iraq crisis on the arising, this Unicor was destined to excel, and excel it did. Every one of us that chose to work in Unicor had to take an industrial sewing course given by Lamar University. It was a sixty-hour course, and I'm happy to say, I was one of the first of the inmates to successfully complete the program. Making me a certified sewer.

Every week or every other week, a bus load of new inmates arrived. And with every bus load, this place began to change. More inmates meant more problems. It wouldn't be long before this place changed into the hell it was designed to become. It had been a little over two weeks since the last bus load of new inmates arrived. This time when it did arrive, it was friends of ours from Indiana getting off the bus.

It was two good friends of ours from New Orleans, so we embraced them both and asked them if they needed anything. It was a normal thing to have what we called a care package (hygiene package) for your homeboys or anyone you knew. Because normally, it takes up to a week or two to get your personal belongings. As we were walking them to their assigned units, they both suddenly stopped and like it was rehearsed, at the same time they asked us had we heard about T-Boy. This caught us both totally off guard, and we looked at one another and said, "What about T-Boy?" They then looked at each other with this puzzled look.

I could tell something was very wrong because of their facial expressions. So when I asked them what was up, one of them told us the whole story. He said about two weeks ago, T-Boy and this white guy got into this heated verbal altercation and when T-Boy turned his back, the white boy struck him in his head with an iron pipe, and he died a few hours later. I couldn't believe what I just was told. My heart was filled with sympathy. I felt like I had gotten news of a close family member being killed. I felt the same degree of pain I felt when I got the news of my cousin being shot and killed.

All I could think about was that eve before my departure when me and my main man T-Boy took our final few laps around that track in Indiana. I remembered us laughing and joking before we embraced and said, "We will be seeing one another soon." Who would have known, that

71

would be the last time I would ever get to look upon the face of my dear friend T-Boy. Fighting to hold back my tears soon proved to be a fight I wouldn't win, as I felt those tears sliding down my cheeks.

A day or two had passed since finding out about T-Boy's death. And with his departure, I somewhat felt obligated to tell my mother about T-Boy. After all, T-Boy wasn't the only one I was keeping a secret from. I had told my mother around a year ago that I was no longer hanging around T-Boy. Because after she learned about him being the one responsible for the gruesome act of arson that caused the deaths of her then boyfriend John's sister-in-law, his niece, and his nephew, and also burned ninety-five percent of his brother's body, but he lived, she begged me to stay away from him, and I told her I would. Yet I never stopped being his friend.

When I finally got ahold of my mother, I told her what had happened to T-Boy and just like déjà vu, my mother seemed to leave the phone. I said, "Mother, Mother, are you there?" Then she said, just like last time, tell John her boyfriend just what I had just told her. And when I did so, though John didn't utter these exact words, his demeanor spoke in volume.

I felt his victory celebration when he said, "Thanks for the news." Who would have known T-Boy's death would represent the greatest degree of sadness from those who truly loved him, as well as a greater degree of satisfaction from those whom held him totally responsible for the loss of their loved ones.

CHAPTER 16

Wide Open

It was only a matter of time before this United States penitentiary became wide open. The last few bus load of inmates had been full of the "badest" of the bad. I mean the worse kind of inmates are now flooding the compound. Yes, this Federal institution is now wide open. They are stepping off the bus looking for shanks which is regular objects turned into insane prison weapons. If it's not weapons they're looking for, it's hooch, or drugs they're wanting. Hooch is homemade alcohol or white lighten which was the purest form of alcohol, which you had to cook, which was not only hard to do without being caught but was equally dangerous because of the possibility of explosion.

Then you had the drugs, the most common being marijuana, then there was cocaine, and heroin. As sad as it may sound, you could purchase either of these drugs as long as you had the money to do so. Of course with this many drugs circulating around, there was bound to be trouble.

It wouldn't be long before the first murder occurred. With this being a new compound, there was always someone trying to control the flow of the drugs. It was now the month of October 1997, and this place was wide open. My only concern was staying out of the way and preparing to see my family soon. I thought by now I would have already seen somebody, but like I stated earlier, I'm still very far from my hometown.

It was around the end of October when this dispute took place between two inmates trying to control the flow of the drugs here. It was said that this inmate from Ohio approached this inmate from Detroit and told him that this compound wasn't big enough for the both of them, and one of them had to go, and it better be him. This really caught the inmate from Detroit off guard, and he took it as the greatest degree of disrespect especially being that he was with his homeboy. To be honest, they both took it as the greatest degree of disrespect and without any warning, they both drew their hidden prison shanks, and when the inmate from Ohio saw this, he proceeded to run. But instead of him running toward the gun tower which would have been the best choice for him, he proceeded to run to his unit.

This would truly prove to be the worse choice of them all because with two inmates after you, there's no way of escaping their wrath. It took only a few minutes before they cornered him off and forcing him into a cell, with their adrenaline flowing out of control, they proceeded to stab him repeatedly, once in the eye socket, the head, the chest, the arms and etc. They then left him for dead, but with the last desperate desire to live, the inmate from Ohio willed his way out of that cell and back outside, walking like a modern-day zombie, before taking his last breath of life then collapsing. The compound was then placed on lock-down and remained that way until a full investigation had took place. Both of the inmates from Detroit was charged with the murder.

The compound is now wide open, any and everything goes. From this moment on, no one is safe or exempt from the possibility of danger. It's already been four fights and two stabbing and now a killing. The compound is just half full, you can only imagine how it will be once at full capacity. What started out as the best institution, in a blink of an eye has turned into a war zone.

Everything has change dramatically, including the way they feed us now. The food went from unbelievable to indescribable. The compound institutional store is now the best thing happening. With every arriving bus load, we were drawn even closer to the hell this place was designed to become. Even the warden himself has now adapted to the new breed of inmates that's now residents of his institution. Yet he refuse to treat them any different. His motto still remains the same, treat the inmates the way you want to be treated.

Talking about wide open, there was nothing you couldn't get a whole of here. I'm talking about from Hooch (homemade alcohol) to any kind of drugs. Of course with the presence of the two, there was always trouble nearby. The best way to stay out of the line of trouble was to stay away from the drugs and alcohol scene. And the best way to do that was to stay as busy as possible. Working in Unicor kept me out of harm's way for the most part, especially with all the overtime we were getting. When I wasn't working, I was coaching or cooking.

They had just started the first flag football league, and I was asked to coach my homeboy that first year. We named our team the Texas Cowboys. All of the players on my team were from Texas. Even though we were halfway full, the league had about eight teams. To name a few you had the Washington Redskins which was the D.C. Cars team, Miami Baller's which was the Florida Cars team. The Saints which was the New Orleans Cars team, The Raiders which was the California team. The Headhunters which was the white boys team. Then you had the Oilers which was another Texas team. Then you had the Bandits which was the Mexican Boys team.

Out of the eight teams, just four of us stood out the strongest. You know with any type of physical contact, there was bound to be trouble. Especially when you're on a wide-open compound. So during the games, there were lots of hard hitting and trash talking. Of course, there would be times when a fight seem to break out in the middle of the field, but with the gun tower standing right there, the fighting never got out of hand. Because everybody knew if it did, someone was going to be shot. No one was fool enough to take it to that level, especially with two armed guards watching over.

CHAPTER 17

When Pure Instinct Takes Over

When pure instinct takes over, there's nothing you can do to stop it. My main goal was to stay out of trouble because that was the only chance I had of giving this life sentence back one day. So I did my best to avoid any kind of altercation. I did a better job of staying out of the line of fire. But in a United States penitentiary, sometimes you just can't escape the unexpected. I've stayed out of the way for five solid years, that within itself is only a blessing from God. You see, in a USP, there's no such thing as turning the other cheek or allowing anyone to disrespect you. Because if you were to ever allow either one of those two acts to happen, you would only be setting yourself up for even more trouble.

Most of the guys here would view such an act as a sign of weakness, and that would open up a door for exploitation either financially or better yet physically. When you're around guys that have lost everything, with nothing to gain, a man that had lost all hopes and dreams, such a man becomes like an animal, or even worse like a monster. Believe me, that's exactly what all United States penitentiaries bred. Yes, there were guys here that watched and waited like vultures for one to show any sign of weakness. You can believe this much about the five years I've been down, anyone that steps to me in such a manner, I would have no choice but to react in a very aggressive manner and would have gratefully accepted the consequence that would have followed.

When I first entered my first USP, I was told by my good friend, a man I called Pops, that if I'm ever approached in a disrespected manner, or if someone raise their hand to harm me, win, lose, or draw, I should automatically react in an aggressive nature. Pops told me that at that exact moment nothing should matter, not even winning. The only thing that matters is that you where man enough to take action. He told me that a man in the USP is not judged by if he wins a fight, or how good of a fighter he is. He is only judged by his willingness to fight for his right to exist as a man.

I truly held on to what I was told by the man I called Pops. Though I did my best to stay out of the line of fire, I was always prepared to defend myself by any means necessary. Even when I wasn't prepared, when pure instinct takes over there's nothing you can do. This was truly the case during lunch time on December 2, 1998. From the time I woke up that day, to the moment all of this took place, pure tension existed. With so much tension in the air, my only goal was to stay out of the way. So I prepared for work and got there as quickly as possible. Because I just knew all hell would be happening at any given moment.

The whispers were everywhere of the coming of trouble. To my surprise, nothing had happened.

It was now lunch time, so I and a couple of my good friends were headed back to the unit for lunch. It was a long walk, and I was still walking with a cane. By the time we reached the unit, I was exhausted, so I stopped at the first TV table. What seemed like seconds later, I heard the biggest commotion. When I turned around to see what was happening, I saw my best friend's homeboy stabbing him with a prison shank (a homemade knife) without hesitation and not even thinking. I rushed toward the two of them, dropping my cane on the way, as I body-blocked his homeboy off him and pulled him away. My best friend's false leg had come off, and this allowed his homeboy the ability to easily straddle him. My best friend had been stabbed in the head and the chest before I was able to knock him off. I will never forget the look his homeboy gave me, he looked at his prison shank in his hand, and then he looked up at me standing there with nothing in mine. I was able to keep him safe until staff members arrived. Yes, my friend did get stabbed a few times, yet I'm sure had I not intervened, he might not be here today.

I quickly thought about dropping my cane, and how crazy that was. When pure instinct takes over, you're truly not in control. My best friend's life was saved because of my instinct. Even though I did a good deed, I was still placed in special housing for two weeks while a full investigation was done. After my best friend explained the role I played, I was released with no charges given. My best friend was so grateful that he wrote a letter on my behalf to my sentencing judge that had given me that life sentence, but as always, we never even got any kind of response. Nevertheless, I truly appreciated him trying. I kept a copy of that letter because of the heartfelt message it carried. Anyway as you can see, sometimes as much as you try to avoid trouble, sometimes you just can't avoid your own instinct.

CHAPTER 18

Unbelievable Moment

We were now 10–0 and headed to the flag prison football playoffs as the number one seed. It was truly an unbelievable moment for the Texas Cowboys, we were on the brink of an undefeated season. And the only team that gave us trouble was the Washington Redskins which was mostly members of the D.C. Car, even though we had beat them both times this year, both games went down to the wire, and could have went either way. We just knew they would be the one we would be facing in the championship game. Not only was it very physical, there was no love lost between the D.C. inmates and the Texas inmates. They were always bumping heads with one another on the field and off the field. So we both knew this game would be personal.

Of course we had the biggest edge, being that this was our home state, so our fan base was three times as big as theirs. So if a riot was to break between the two of us, we had the numbers, and they knew this. At the same time, the D.C. Car showed no fear, mainly because they were true warriors, and they were very skilled fighters especially with a prison shank in their hands. So we all knew that even though our numbers were more, they weren't to be taken lightly.

Just as expected, we both ended up playing for the prison Super Bowl. This game not only gained the attention of most of the inmates on this compound, but it also gained the attention of the staff members, mainly because they were very aware of the strong possibility of a riot breaking out at any given moment between the two teams, so they made sure they had extra staff members at the game. At the same time, a game of this magnitude drew the interest of many, including most of the executive staff members, such as the warden himself.

As always, it was a very tight game. Matter of fact, the Redskins led us at halftime 14 to 8. The second half was even more tighter. No one had scored, and it was only five minutes left in the game. Trailing by six, our chances of winning were slim. We would have to score a touchdown to even tie the game, and then we would have to convert a two-point play to win the game because there was no field goal kicking in flag football here.

With only seconds left, we decided to put the ball in the hands of our best player, Swan, he was the best wide receiver on the compound, and the D.C. Boys knew we would be getting him the ball, but this time, instead of throwing it to him, I called this unexpected play, a triple reverse with him getting the ball last, it was truly an unbelievable moment when he got the ball in his hand, he ran around the back field for what seemed like one minute before exploding down the sideline for a thirty-yard touchdown to tie the game with twenty seconds left. Our sideline went buzzard, cheering like *crazy*. Everyone ran to the end zone, the football players and our fans.

Once the field was cleared, we went for the win. Swan was spread wide right and the other two receivers was spread wide left. They just knew this would be a pass play to Swan, but this time I called a quarterback draw, and Dre Money strolled into the end zone untouched as time ran out, giving us a victory score of sixteen to fourteen. It was the greatest unbelievable moment I had ever experienced, my arms were full of chill bumps. At that moment, I was as free as I have ever been.

The cheering was so loud that I knew it could be heard for miles and miles. The chant "Na na na. Na na na na. Hey, hey, hey, goodbye," went on for what seemed like thirty minutes straight. The Texas Cowboys would go on to win a consecutive seven prison Super Bowls in a row. Though there were no records kept, as far as I know this has never been done throughout the history of the Federal system, and I'm sure the Texas Cowboys still holds the record of consecutive prison Super Bowl wins as of today.

Months were truly flying by before I knew it. Another flag football season was right around the corner. But the only thing that was on my mind was the news I received just a week ago. It's been one year and two months and seven days since I arrived here in Texas, and I still haven't seen any of my family members. But last week, my sister told me that she and my cousin was coming down this coming weekend, and they would be staying the whole weekend. Man, I hadn't seen my big sister for over ten years because she was staying in Memphis when I was out there.

I know it's going to be a very emotional reunion because my sister is so much like my mother, they both are very emotional people and will drop a tear in a New York second. So I have to prepare to see her because if I don't, we will both be out there crying a river. I really don't know what to expect because it's been so many years since I've seen my big sister. I was hoping she would be bringing my mother, but this time it won't be happening. My big brother promised me he would be bringing her soon. Yes, I happen to be the baby boy of the three of us. My mother and father had four kids but she lost her second during a miscarriage, it was a boy.

My mother and father divorced when I was a baby. They both got remarried, and we were blessed with a half brother and three half sisters from my father. The young lady that was coming with my sister had a baby by one of my favorite cousins who was shot to death at a party. We were very close, he was the one that taught me how to drive a stick shift. His death was the first one I had to endure, and it was very painful. Just thinking about him not being there cause my heart so much sorrow still. During that time, having this life sentence didn't seem all that bad.

On July 18, 1998, I was called to my first visit. As I entered the visiting room, my heart was racing out of control. After so many years, I didn't know what to expect. Within seconds, I saw this beautiful slim ebony queen running in my direction. As she got closer and closer, her precious smile let me know just who she was. Her tears had already started to flow from those beautiful big eyes, as she screamed out, "My brother. Oh my, brother." As she leaped into my arms, I can't say who held on the tightest, but I do know that neither one of us wanted to let go. This was truly an unbelievable moment, and I still cherish that moment as if it happened yesterday.

Finally, I got to hug my cousin. She was just as happy, and tears found their way to her eyes as well. I than sat between the two of them, and we talked and hugged the whole visit. I made sure I had plenty of picture tickets, we took about ten pictures together. I also had them to take a couple by themselves, so I could show them off to the guys. The rest we took together. The visit went by so, so fast, and when it was time to say goodbye, my sister cried like a baby. But I made her laugh, and I reminded her that we will be seeing each other tomorrow. I was on cloud nine leaving the visiting room.

The next two visits went the exact same way, and I mean to the letter. My sister would run up to me and cry every single time, and when it was time to leave, she did the same thing. Every visit was just like déjà vu. We talked and hugged the whole visit and took lots of pictures. I will admit that the last goodbye was a little more intense. I even shed a tear or two. I couldn't thank God enough for this unbelievable moment.

CHAPTER 19

No Stopping

There was no stopping this place from becoming the hell it was designed to become. The strong presence of tension was simply a part of the prison. There was no stopping its presence. Everywhere you went you felt it. You had to speed walk everywhere you went, just to make sure if something went down, you were in a safe place. Well, what you would call a safe place because to be honest, such a place didn't exist. The only place that would come close to making you feel safe was in your own cell, and even then you would have to rig your door so no one could get in.

There was just no stopping the violence and the drugs. I guess when you have lots of people with so much time, and no sight of relief coming, what else is to be expected. Though I carry the same type of time, I refuse to become a lesser man. I refuse to fall prey to the system's true intentions. They want you to bury yourself deeper, so if by chance relief does come your way, you won't be able to take advantage of that opportunity because of your past behavior.

When you're doing time in a United States penitentiary, there's just so many things to watch out for. It's so easy to fall prey to one of those prison traps because they are everywhere, and they come in many different disguises. The simplest thing such as shutting a staff member's office door when they have left it unprotected could cause you your life. This is an example of one of those many prison traps that awaits that unaware inmate. A trap even I have once fell prey to.

Let us not leave out the presence of prison peer pressure, for you will find the worse kind in a United States penitentiary. I witness its effects with my own two eyes. I was standing in the institution store line, when I saw this young white gang member attack this other older white inmate. He chased him right up to E Building front entrance, right out of the sight of the gun tower. The staff members saw the altercation and proceeded to it.

When they got there, they saw this young gang member with this very large prison shank in his hand. He was trying to stab this older inmate, but the older inmate had fallen onto his back and was spinning around kicking up at the other inmate, trying his best to keep him from being able to stab him in any vital part of his body.

The young gang member was a little too fast, and yes he managed to stab him repeatedly on every part of his body. By now more staff members had arrived, and they had fully circled the both of them, yet they still refuse to take actions. The older inmate finally lost conscience, and when he did, the young inmate stabbed him one more time then he dropped the knife. The staff members then attacked him all at once, while the older man laid there dead. I just couldn't believe what I had just witness. They actually watched one inmate kill another, and they did nothing.

I heard days later that the older inmate owed the young gang member money. Money that the older inmate had assured him it had been sent. But when it didn't arrive on the day it supposed to have, some of the young boys gang members convinced him that he was being played, and he should make a statement. Prison peer pressure at its best. Even though the young gang member only had a few more months to do before going home, he allowed prison peer pressure to get the best of him. It was no stopping him after that. The sad part about it all, the next day he received the money on his books.

Now he's facing a life sentence and will most likely spend the rest of his life in prison. After the week-long lockdown. I saw one of the staff officers that was on the scene when that killing took place, and I went up to him and asked him why did they do nothing to save that inmate's life, and he simply said that no staff member there was willing to risk being stabbed or killed to save an inmate. I'm so sure had it been one of his own being stabbed, there would have been no stopping them.

CHAPTER 20

A Time to Reflect

With all of this madness, a time to reflect always seems to provide me with some very needed tranquility. You have to try your best to find your own way because if you don't, you will mostly find yourself neck deep in a bad situation. And if that's not the case, you will most likely find yourself on the brink of insanity. It's so easy to lose your own way. Believe me, I've seen it happen. I've seen guys pushed so hard that when night came, they took their own life. I saw them become so afraid that they would rather play like a woman than to remain being a man.

Rather they knew it or not, the system creates these fatal conclusions. Just think about it. They give you a horrific amount of time, then they place you all together. They cage you like animals and feed you slop. They put all type of limitations on you, and then they expect you to act like something other than the animal they have created you to be. A time to reflect helps you to see beyond the system, beyond its madness. When I reflect, I see and I hear my mother and father. I see my kids running to me calling out, "Daddy. Daddy."

I see and hear freedom calling me home. I hear my big brother telling me, "Man, I can't wait for you to come home." I hear my big sister following suit brother we need you here.

Yes, when I reflect, I see clearly what the system wants me to miss. A time to reflect gives me the power to overcome. It helps me to see beyond this life sentence. It reminds me of others that has endured even worse. I think about those starving kids in Africa, that's forced to drink the foulest of water.

I then realized how blessed I still am even with a life sentence. I have no idea of when freedom will be coming for me, but I do know this much. I'll be ready. You've got to stay ready in order to be ready. Meaning, you have to keep your head raised high, and you can't show any kind of weakness. You pray every night for peace, but you stay ready for war. Remember, a battle is only lost if you refuse to defend yourself when you're forced to do so.

It's been more than five years now, and I have yet to lift one hand against another, nor have one hand been lifted against me. It's not because I'm bad or anyone fears me. I just know how to mind my own business. I know how to treat people. I just treat them the way I want to be treated. The main things I don't do is drink or do drugs, nor would I advise one to gamble because those three things could keep you in harm's way. Now I'm way from being perfect because I do gamble. I just try my best to keep it in perspective.

Well, it's now rolling into 1999, and the Texas Cowboys have won its second prison Super Bowl. Time is really moving on. I'm really hoping to see my mother and brother soon. Sometimes this time gets the best of me, but when I reflect, I always snap back.

You have to keep your faith and stay focus and before you know it, freedom will be calling out your name. A time to reflect opens so many doors, and you can see so many changes. My kids are sounding like grownups when I call, yet they still ask me the same question, "When are you coming home?" And I always tell them maybe next year.

My youngest daughter had the nerve to say, "Daddy, you always say that." My reply is always the same, "Well, baby, Daddy always feel that way." The last time I saw my baby girl, she was jumping up and down in that visiting room window. Now she's talking like a big girl, and she's only seven. Believe me, not knowing when your time is up really weighs heavy on the heart. This life sentence isn't a joke. But I've made up in my mind that if I'm going to be here for some years, you can believe this much, I'm going to take very good care of myself. The first thing I did was to give up eating pork, and I did so for health reasons only. Hey, I loved pork, but it's just not good for me.

When you have a time to reflect, you have time to correct yourself, to prepare yourself, to better yourself. You have time to right your wrongs. For the most part, when you have time to reflect, especially in my present state of condition, you can really see those who are really there for you.

CHAPTER 21

Still Hoping

With this being President Bill Clinton's last term, we were all sure he would be helping us. At least, we were all still hoping that would be the case. But instead, on March 24, 1999, the United States and NATO began a major aircraft bombing of Serbia. The only good thing about this was the business this Unicor got from this act of war. Being that we specialized in putting together Army fatigue, business at this Unicor was booming. Overtime was plentiful and this really kept those who worked in Unicor out of the mixed.

Yet I was still hoping this would be my year. I wanted so badly to see my grandmother and my great aunt, who were two sisters that stayed together for as long as I could remember. My grandmother and her sister as far as I've known have never been apart. So I grew up with them both. My grandmother had two daughters and my great aunt had two daughters and four sons. With them always living together, this made us a very tight-knit family.

I was still hoping that I would not only get to see the two of them, I was also hoping to see my other grandmother on my daddy's side. Plus I wanted to see my granddaddy. I know he wasn't my blood granddaddy, but he was the one my daddy introduced us as our granddaddy when we were little, so I always treated him like my own granddad, and as far as I'm concern that's just who he was. I love him just as much as I love my grandmothers and my great aunt.

They were the ones I really thought about seeing the most because I knew because of their ages, they could be gone at any given moment. My mother and father was also getting up in age. I always pray to God to please let me get out of here before anything happens to my mother because my mother truly carries the torch for my big sister and my big brother. If something was to happen to her, they both would be lost. You see, though I'm the baby boy of the family, I've always been like the older brother to them both.

So I just knew I would be the one to continue to carry that torch, just as if I was my mother. I'm still praying daily for that blessing. Time seems to be moving super fast. That would be a good thing if only I had a date. No one out there can truly understand how it feels to not know your future outcome. A Federal life sentence comes with no parole. Even though I have camp points due to my good behavior, the life sentence still holds me in a high-level institution. I've been told that once I've done ten years or better with good behavior, I can put in for a transfer to an FCI, which would be a medium Federal Correctional Institution. It would be like leaving hell and going to heaven.

You see, guys that go to an FCI, especially after doing time in a United States Penitentiary, never want to come back. Guys that have never been here never want to come because of all the horrific stories they have heard. For the most part, the inmates at an FCI is on their best behavior. So you don't see killings or much stabbings. Yes, there's a few fist fights here and there, but nothing more for the most part.

I'm still hoping my brother will keep his word and bring my mother soon. It's been a whole year since he made me that promise. But I truly understand how it is out there. With working all this overtime at Unicor and coaching my Texas Cowboys. I'm really keeping myself busy. Yes, we are going for the three peat. Hey, I just got off the phone with my brother, and he was asking me some strange questions. Questions like what I am going to be doing this weekend, and how far is this institution from Houston. When I asked him why all these type of questions, he just changed the subject.

Hey, that sounds like a surprise visit in the making. Even though we hate surprise visit because we have to have the time to get ourselves together. So just to be on the safe side, I got all the way ready. I got my hair cut, I got my clothes ironed, and I got my picture tickets ready. Even though I really didn't know if it was going to happen. I was still hoping it would.

Sure enough, on October 10, 1999 on a Sunday, I was called to visit that week later. I just knew it was my brother and mother, at least I was hoping it would be. With my heart fluttering, I stepped through the visiting door. Like I said before, my mother is a very emotional person, so I was expecting plenty of tears. But what I got was the opposite. My brother's little daughter was the one to run up to me first after my brother told her there's your uncle. Even though this was our first-time meeting, she showed no fear as she made her way into my arms.

My brother and his wife followed suit with their own firm embracement. The whole while my mother sat there staring at me with the most beautiful smile, not saying a word.

I just knew the tears was on their way. After all, it's been seven long years since we last saw one another, and even then it was during my trial, so that wasn't a good memory for either one of us. As I looked at my mother just as hard, I saw my grandmother. All I could do was smile. Finally, my mother found her way into my arms. I could feel her heart racing a hundred mile an hour, and my own even faster. I felt like a baby in my mother's arms, and it took everything inside of me not to shed a thousand tears. My mother never let me go, and she never looked away from me. We sat right next to each other, and she held on to my arm.

She kept on touching my face and my head. Even when it was time to take pictures, she refused to look into the camera, she would only look at me and say, "My baby. Look at my baby." But what she didn't do was shed one single tear. I was so glad of that because I knew if she would have, there would have been no stopping my own tears. The visit went as fast as it came. It was truly the greatest moment ever. As the visit ended, saying our goodbyes was one of my saddest moments, but I showed no sadness, I showed only happiness as I held my mother for that final moment. I could see her fighting off the tears as she was walking away, but one single tear fought even harder to escape. As I exited the visiting room, I was left still hoping for the day freedom calls me home.

CHAPTER 22

Could This Be the End

After seeing my mother, I was riding on a cloud so large that I couldn't look down. I was feeling a joy like no other. Nothing that was going on around me bothered me. I was truly in my own little world. Then came the talk of the coming of the new millennium. You would have thought this would be a great coming event, but it was truly the opposite. I heard that when the new millennium gets here, it could be the ending of the world as we know of it today. To be honest, this was truly a blessing in disguise if you were to ask someone doing this kind of time. Yes, we were all looking forward to the change because as far as most of us were concern, life couldn't get any worse. Could this really be the end?

I'm telling you, when talk about the ending coming, you should see all the craziness that comes with it. I mean you have people really trying to prepare for the end. All the talk really had to do with the Y2K Scare. It was about all the computers crashing all at once, which would virtually take us back to the stone ages. As this day quickly approaches, the world was truly in a panic. The come-to-meet-Jesus talk was at it's all time high. The world was actually afraid of something other than a war. Could this be the end? Of course most of us here never took any of this talk seriously because as far as we were concern, the world ended the day we received such harsh punishments, especially for me. What could be worse than a life sentence. To be honest, we were all hoping the computers all went down because then maybe they would lose all of our case info and be forced to lessen our sentences.

While the world prepared for the end, us inmates rejoiced the possibility of a needed change, and if it took the so-called coming of the end to get it, we were all down for it. Yes, we were all caught up in the hype. It was also the election year, but the Y2K talk got most of the attention. But that didn't mean the inmates weren't paying close attention to the poles. Matter of fact, we were all pulling for Al Gore, and it was looking like we would be getting our wish. Even though Bill Clinton did very little for us during his eight-year stay.

We felt that Gore would be better than another Bush. Even with all that was going on, we still made time to get our loved ones out to vote. With the coming of every presidential election year, there was always a thought of hope that a new president would see the need of sentencing reform. And as far as we were all concern, Al Gore was our man.

When the clock struck 12:00 a.m. at that highly anticipated moment, you could hear that sigh of relief throughout the universe when absolutely nothing happened. On the other hand, us inmates, we were all disappointed. Matter of fact, most of us stayed up just to see what was going to happen. All the madness had ended just as fast as it had started, and the world resumed as normal. Could this be the end? The answer to that question was not this time around. You know truth be told, most of us knew nothing like that would happen, and yes we wanted the Y2K talk to be true because it really would have brought about a much-needed change especially for people doing this degree of time.

Yet it was back to business as usual. The same ole same ole. The US jobless rate was at its lowest in twenty-five years. The Olympic Games opened in Australia. Three astronauts reached the international space station for the first time. And yes the Texas Cowboys did go on to win its third consecutive prison Super Bowl. But the biggest news of the year 2000 is when our Al Gore got ambushed by Florida's Bush, giving his brother George Jr. that needed push back into the White House. Could this be the end? As far as sentencing reform goes, with Bush in control, it is as close to the end as it could get when you're doing this type of time because we can expect no changes being made with Bush in office. This year came and went. We rolled into the next year just as fast.

But what took place almost at the end of 2001 would haunt the hearts of many. No one was prepared for that unbelievable moment. It was a Tuesday morning around 8:46 a.m. when the whole world witness the greatest catastrophe of this time. At this very moment ever, souls cried out contemporaneously. For the first time in many years, every race, creed, or color stood as one in prayer. September 11, 2001 is truly a day that will haunt us for as long as we live.

CHAPTER 23

Another Day but the Same Ole Way

Yes, it's another day, but the same ole way is still happening. There's fighting, and guys are still being stabbed, the drug trade is still on the rise, and death is always right around the corner. A beef between two gang rivals could escalate into a full-fledged riot an a drop of a dime. This was truly the case when a disagreement between a gangster disciple and a member of the D.C. Car had words that turned into a fight. Though the fight was broke up and the two that was involved in the fight had been taken into custody, that still did not put out the fire. For on the very next day, a strategic attack was planned and orchestrated out simultaneously within every unit by members of the D.C. Car.

Yes, a distress call went out throughout the institution. Staff members were running around like their heads where cut off because before they could get to one distress call, another unit was sending out the same distress call. There was a total of twelve units and a distress call was coming from them all. More staff members was called in from the other surrounding institutions because of the magnitude of these incidents. The whole institution was quickly placed on lockdown, and it was weeks before things were back to normal. There were stabbings and fighting throughout the whole institution, and it was truly a very bloody day. Yet to everyone's surprise, there was not one fatal casualty.

When a situation of this magnitude takes place, the lockdown last a little longer because all parties involved will automatically be transferred to other institutions. If too many are involved, they will simply transfer either all of the gang members of the Gangster Disciples or all the members of the D.C. Car. It's normally the gang with the less members that are transferred. This time around, that happened to be the Gangster Disciples gang members that got transferred. The D.C. Car members were allowed to stay, of course they all spent a couple of months in the institutional detention center before being gradually placed back into general population.

Yes, it was another day but always the same ole way. I truly cherished the few days when things appeared to be quiet around here. Yet just because you couldn't hear anything didn't mean noise wasn't still being made. Life in a US penitentiary automatically comes with constant acts of violence mixed with chaos and confusion.

There's simply no way around the madness that comes with doing time in any United States penitentiary. To escape its madness, you have to leave its environment totally. Simply going to another United States penitentiary won't change a single thing. Please believe me when I say they are all the same. Yes, some are a little worse than the other, yet they all carry the title of *bad.*

With the type of time we were all given, most of us will be forced to live our life in such an environment for at least ten years or better. If we happen to reach the ten-year period with good behavior, then we could be transferred to a medium institution. Such an institution is known as an FCI (Federal Correctional Institution), which happens to be medium security. The difference between the two is like night and day, at least that's what I've been told. I can't speak by experience because I have never been. All my seven years have been spent in United States penitentiaries. I'm praying that one day, I will get to experience a life without all the violence and chaos and confusion. Surely that will represent a certain degree of freedom without being free.

Yes, another day but the same ole way is truly the life I'm forced to live. Yet my eyes are always on that light, and I pray constantly for the day I can change these same ole ways.

CHAPTER 24

My Hell. My Fight.

Yes, this is my hell, my fight. From the time I decided to go down that wrong path until the day I was given this life sentence, my hell, my fight began. I'm man enough to admit I committed the first wrong. I made a lot of bad choices, and I created my own hell along the way. A lot of times I tried to blame it on losing a job or the needs of my loved ones.

I would even bring up the fact that I am a black man or just how I was raised. It was so easy to justify the making of those bad choices. Now I'm living the hell I created, and it's my fight and my fight alone. My father or mother can't fight my fight, even though they wish they could.

At the same time, they too can feel the hell I live. I'm so saddened by that fact. Had I really thought about the effect this would have on my whole family, I would have never made those bad choices. It's so easy to see so clearly when you're looking from hell. I'm living a nightmare, a nightmare I created. So often I call upon God asking why must I endure such degree of pain and suffering? Yet even in my hell, I'm constantly reminded of *his* many blessings.

Each day I'm awaken is truly a blessing from *God*. For there're many who are no longer on this earth to receive such a blessing.

God has bestowed upon me the ability to reach one's heart through their stomach. This has served as a shield of protection over me. It's been eight years now and I have yet to encounter any type of physical or verbal altercations. My cooking ability allows me to serve many that's missing home-cooked meal. And I discriminate against no one.

Everyone is welcome to eat from my menu. All the leaders of every gang look forward to one of my many meals. I quickly learned that when you're a very good cook, you have very little reason to fear any harm coming your way. Believe me, when you can cook like someone's grandmother or mother, no harm will ever come your way. There's no substitute for a satisfied appetite.

My hell, my fight, my cooking, my might. My weapon is the microwave and from it, is where I create magical meals such as my special southern fried chicken, fried noodles, meat loaf, chicken and dumplings, southern fried fish, fried onion rings, fried mackerel, jumbo turkey legs, nacho burrito supreme, gumbo, and more. One time there was one of my southern fried leg quarters left and so many guys wanted it that they started a bidding war. And that one fried leg quarter went for ten dollars. The winner said he would have paid whatever, and it was well worth every penny.

With working in Unicor and cooking, plus coaching my Texas Cowboys alone, with running one of the biggest prison stores, it made my hell tolerable. The years seemed to fly by even though I had no date. My hell, my fight, my legacy. I had established myself as being one of the best cooks in the federal system and just as good of a flag football coach. My Texas Cowboys would go on to win seven consecutive prison Super Bowls in a row, and that is truly an unheard-of accomplishment. I had also earned the highest of honors within Unicor. I went from being a sewer to being a lead man in my section. I went from regular pay to premium pay, which is the highest pay level one could accomplish within the Unicor System. Out of 350 inmates that worked in Unicor, it was only six premium pay grades given out.

Even with all of my credentials, there was still the possibility of becoming a victim at any given moment. No one was exempt from that possibility. My hell, my fight came with no ending in sight.

CHAPTER 25

A Blessing Given Back

God has truly blessed me during my time here and everywhere else. The question I used to ask *him* all the time I don't ask *him* so often no more. Because I see *his* answer daily. I used to ask *God* why. Why all of this time, why all of this suffering. I'm really coming to understand that of *his* mission for me. There's been so many lives I've touched as well as saved. And I'm not talking just about the guys locked up. I'm also talking about the lives of the people that I've met that are out there in the land of the free.

Everyone knows that this isn't the place for one to build a debt. But you have guys here with drug habits that does just that. And when their bill gets too big, they can easily lose their lives behind a few dollars. When you're running one of the biggest prison stores in the system, you're in the position to bless those in need, even if that need isn't right. At the same time, sometimes you have to look beyond the cause to prevent the outcome. So I choose to return the blessings that I had received, and to help as many as I could. When I paid a debt, I would always talk to both parties together, and I would explain to the dealer that I'm paying him this time, and for him not to sell drugs to this guy no more, and if he does, when he knows the guy with a habit can't pay him, he better except it as a lost. Because he's been warned.

Sometimes they listen, and sometimes they don't. So I end up seeing the two of them again. Sometimes I did get paid back, but for the most part, I charged it to the game. I was also able to help my mother get her home and help my brother when he did some state time. So even though I was serving a life sentence, I was still able to make a difference in a lot of people's lives. I always had a lot of pen pals and at times, you wouldn't know who was the one doing time by listening to our conversation because I was always the one with the upbeat personality, and I was the one with a life sentence.

One of the biggest blessing I was able to return came when I was blindsided by one of the biggest surprises. Now it's not uncommon for you to run across a person you met in another institution, especially if you're from the same region. But to run across someone that's not from your state is very rare. This was the case when out of nowhere came one of the guys I met in Indiana when I went to my first United States Penitentiary. I can honestly say that through his teaching, I was able to survive the madness, not only there but also here. He taught me so much, and he was always there for me. He treated me like a son, and there was nothing he wouldn't have done for me.

He was like a father, and I called him Pops. Way from St. Louis came a man I hadn't seen in years. A man that had taught me everything. A man that was always there for me. This time he's the one far from home, he's the one with very few homeboys around. The lifestyle he was accustomed then might not be possible here. At least that's what he may have assumed. You see, Pops was the type of man that liked to be needed. He was a people's person. God had put me in the position to return the blessings that Pops had given unto me. I have ran one of the biggest stores in the system for years, and I'm really tired. What better person to pass this on to than the man I called Pops.

When I saw Pops, we embraced, and we both were very happy to see one another. We talked forever. A few weeks later, I told him about my plans to turn over my store business to him, and he was so pleased and excited. Right away, he went into action, making himself known as the new inmate store man. It made me so happy to see the joy in his eyes. Who could have known I would be in the position to give back such a blessing to the man I called Pops. A man that taught me how to survive this type of horrific lifestyle. A man that went out of his way to make sure I was safe. Even though he knew nothing about me. I was truly blessed to run across such a man. God knows it's not often such a blessing come to one in these conditions.

It took the manpower of four to five of us to transfer my store. My store inventory exceeded over a couple of thousands. To me that still wasn't enough, but you couldn't tell my Pops that. He was overly pleased. And that was good enough for me.

CHAPTER 26

Another Beginning

The latest talk has been the opening of this FCI in Mississippi. A notice have been placed in every unit stating that if you have been a modest inmate, you can put in a transfer request to the new institution. Yes, I know you may be asking yourself why would I even consider transferring out of my home state when I could transfer across the street to the FCI next door. Truth be told, it's been more trouble over there than any other FCI I've heard about. So if I'm going to start another beginning, I would rather it be in an FCI I get to help open. There's nothing like being the first ones there.

My main reason for wanting to leave is the need to get out of the United States Penitentiary environment. I'm so tired of all the killing and madness. But what really put the icing on the cake was what took place on this sunny Saturday. We were all outside watching a championship baseball game when I was approached and told that there was a body up under one of the bunks in the C-4 Unit. This news spread like a wildfire, at least to the inmates. The one thing about the USP, the inmates were always the first to know about what's going to go down and what has gone down. Because everyone knows once the officers find out, we are automatically placed on lockdown. The heads up gave us the time to get the things we need done. Like canceling a visit that may have been planned or get the things you need, like stamps or commissary from an inmate store man.

Not to mention getting a hot shower in because once you are placed on lockdown, there's no telling when they will allow us to take a shower. It wasn't all that bad because we do have a sink in our room, so a birdbath was very much the thing to do during a lengthy lockdown. There was one other person that wouldn't be told about this killing, and that was the guy that lived with the victim. Everyone was avoiding him just like he had a plague. Because everyone knew that he would be the first one questioned, and no one wanted to take the chance of him implementing them into the equation.

The anticipation of the outcome of this whole event took on a life of its own. Everyone was anxious to see the reaction of the guy who would soon discover his dead celly's body who had been lying underneath his own bunk. He should have been able to feel all the eyes that were watching his every move. In the common area, there were about five TVs with inmates sitting around them all, but not one inmate was paying any attention to the TVs.

As the older inmate got closer to his cell door, every eye was on him. It took only a few moments after he entered his cell before the panic button was ignited. Every cell had a panic button for emergency purpose only. Once the panic button was ignited, the unit officer moved quickly to the cell. Soon after his entrance, he immediately hit the deuces. (Deuces is a button located on all officers walkie-talkies). Every officer on duty had to respond, and that they did. The whole institution was placed on lockdown. To everyone's surprise, there were two gurneys headed to that cell. One for the dead body, and another one for the old man that had passed out after hitting the panic button. The next morning, a ten member forensic team was brought in.

The word around the institution for the reason behind the murder was that the guy was a snitch that had just step off the bus only hours ago. We later learned that he had been stabbed sixty-nine times or so. All I knew was it was time for another beginning, and this time it would be at an FCI. I simply had to do what was best for me. I knew my family wouldn't agree with the move at first, but after I explained to them where I was going and how safer I would be, they would be all for the move. Especially after they hear about what just took place. My mind as well as my heart began to race with enthusiasm with the mere thought of finally going to an FCI after spending twelve long years in bloody USPs. Yes, this would be another institution I would be opening, but this time, everyone coming will be inmates that has earned the right to be here, or inmates that are already at medium custody. It was one thing for certain, another beginning at a new FCI would be like leaving hell and going to heaven. I was truly overdue for such an experience.

CHAPTER 27

Moving On Up

I had put in for the new FCI in Mississippi a couple of weeks ago, and I was told by my unit team that I had been approved for the transfer. There's not a lot to rejoice over when you're serving a life sentence, but this news today brought the greatest joy to my heart, and I was so ready for the change. But there was one wish I still wanted and that was to see my mother before I left. So I called my brother and asked him if he would bring my mother to see me, and he said he would. That brought even more joy to my heart. Not only would I get to see my mother, but I would get to see my brother as well. What a wonderful way to be leaving.

For the most part, I kept my leaving on the down low because it wasn't too wise to share that kind of information, at least not to everyone. Because sometimes, there just may be someone that would rather you stay right where you are. So they would either start a fight with you or go as far as planting a weapon or whatever in your property. Either one of these acts would hinder you from being transferred. So to be on the safe side, it was best for you to keep quiet about transferring. I only shared my leaving with my closest friends. All I could think of was moving on up. I even dreamed about how it would be. There were so many signs letting me know it was time for this move. One of those signs was when my Texas Cowboys finally lost their first prison Super Bowl. But hey, what a run we had. It's going to be impossible for anyone to top our seven consecutive prison Super Bowl wins in a row at that.

I couldn't thank God enough for keeping me safe as well as healthy. Not to mention finally getting me out of this environment. Yet as much as I was ready to go, the bond I had built with so many here weighed on my heart. Because for eight years, this was my residence, and they were my family. I truly loved my brothers, and they all will be truly missed. This was a very long stay and even with all the madness at times, there were moments of happiness that could never be replaced. A total of twelve years in United States Penitentiaries and finally I'm moving on up.

It has been close to six years since I last saw my mother or any of my family members. But it really didn't feel like those many years had passed since the last time I saw them. Nevertheless, I was ready to see them. When that day finally arrived, my heart was racing. The joy was like no other as I entered the visiting room. It was truly like déjà vu again. My little niece, well, my now big girl niece ran up to me and gave me the biggest hug. My brother and his wife followed suit. My mother sat there patiently waiting on her turn. As I looked upon her motherly beauty, I saw my grandmother Madea, and all kind of childhood memories raced through my mind. How grateful I felt when I was blessed to see both the women I loved sitting in that same chair.

My mother's embracement made me feel five years old all over again. Then came my grandmother's embracement, my Madea. I recalled our last conversation over the phone, and I told my grandmother to hold on because I would be coming home soon, and she said she would and that she loved me. Even though a few months later, she passed away. Yet all I can now say is that she kept her word, for today she lives on within the soul of her daughter. The visit went as fast as it came, but the joy it brought have yet to leave my heart. I can't thank God enough for *his* many blessings, and now I'm ready for *his* next mission.

CHAPTER 28

My First F.C.I.

It's always hard saying goodbye to all of your brothers, but when it's time to go, there's nothing else to be said. That doesn't make it any easier. It's just hard saying goodbye to the guys you've been around for eight long years. Most of them are truly like family. As I took a glance back into time, I could see all the good that has transpired. I see the hearts I've touched and the lives I may have saved. I'm then reminded of the blessings God has given unto me. The power of protection he continues to bless me with. This enables me to see beyond this life sentence, beyond this darkness. He enables me to see that light to my freedom.

He's now blessed me to see my first F.C.I. (Federal Correctional Institution) which takes me all the way out of harm's way. Like I said before, leaving a United States penitentiary and going to a Federal correctional institution is like leaving hell and going to heaven. And to make it even more of a blessing, I get the chance to be one of the first to set the tone in this new Federal correctional institution. Just think about it. I was a part of opening the first United States penitentiary in the State of Texas. It was truly one of the greatest experiences I've had while doing this time. Now I get to do it all over again but this time, the preparation is for the coming of those who have earned the right to be here, or for those who are already at medium custody.

I had said all my goodbyes, and I was now on the bus headed to my first F.C.I. in the State of Mississippi. That early morning when I was called to leave, I had already packed out a couple of days ago. As I was walking across the prison yard, I looked up to see the moon and the early morning stars. I was quickly brought back to reality, as the gun tower interrupted my view. I could see the shadow of the officer and his assault rifle as he watched our every move. Yes, it was numerous of us leaving that early morning.

That was truly a sight I wouldn't be missing. As we boarded the bus shackled from waist to feet, I was lost in thought. As the bus exited its final barbed-wired fence. I dared to look back. This biblical story came right to my thoughts. It was about Lot's wife turning into a pillar of salt after she looked back at Sodom.

To my surprise, I wouldn't be flying to Mississippi, instead it would be a long bus ride and that it was. To make matter worse, it began to rain cats and dogs. I was sitting close to the front, and it was raining so hard I couldn't see out of the front window, and I was surely wondering how in the hell could the driver see, especially at the rate of speed he was going. To a man that hadn't been in a car or a bus for the last eight years, I was on the verge of having a heart attack. It got so bad I just had to try to make myself go to sleep. My biggest fear came when we cross this body of water that appeared to be even with the bridge we were on. But did that stop the driver from going so fast, no it did not. I was beginning to wonder if I would make it to my first F.C.I. I really forced myself to sleep.

Hours later, I was awaken by the subtle stop of the bus. All I could do was thank God we had safely made it to my first F.C.I. I let out a sigh of relief that was so loud it almost got me in trouble. As I stepped off the bus, I felt something I hadn't felt in years, it was truly a feeling that was hard to describe, but if I had to put it in words, I would say "At peace." For the first time in years, there was not even the possibility of tension existing anywhere in this institution. One of the biggest reasons why was the fact that there was only a few inmates here. It was a total of twelve units, and the inmates that was there housed just one of those units, and we were all placed in that same unit.

As we were walking to that unit, I noticed the similar features this new F.C.I. had like the U.S.P. I had just left. But what brought me out of that thought was when there was no gun tower present. That alone brought a sense of comfort like no other. When we finally got to our unit, I heard nothing but laughter and joy. It was like we walked into a party atmosphere. You couldn't do nothing but smile. As I looked upon the thirty or so inmates that was in the unit, I couldn't find not one that appeared to be a threat. I really didn't know how long this feeling would last but I was determined to hold on to it as long as I could. As far as I could see, everything that I had heard about the F.C.I. was true.

CHAPTER 29

Still Popping

When coming from such a horrific atmosphere in the likes of United States penitentiaries, it was very easy to underestimate the peaceful atmosphere of an F.C.I. At the same time, *prison* is *prison* and it's still popping, no matter where you are, it has its own way of letting you know just that. That was exactly the case on this particular day during the latter part of summer 2005. It seem like it was only yesterday when there was only a small number of inmates here, now within a few months we were on the verge of a full capacity institution. I can recall seeing busloads of inmates coming in daily, and sometimes two busloads a day. I knew it wouldn't be long before we were at maximum capacity. Even with so many here, the atmosphere remained peaceful. It was truly a different breed of inmates. At the same time, there was also a few of us that had earned our way out of the U.S.P.

And not everyone of us was truly transformed out of that U.S.P. mentality. That could also lead to a lot of manipulation. You have to understand that coming from a U.S.P. gives one the upper hand verses one that has never been. It also gives one that has been to the U.S.P. a certain degree of respect automatically. What took place on this particular hot summer day would be viewed by most as a horrific event. An event that really very seldom happens in an F.C.I. To be honest, you can add the hot weather factor to this event as well because I truly feel that it played a major role in the manifestation of this horrific event. Still popping was an understatement on this particular day.

It was just too hot for me to be hanging out outside plus I had been waiting for us to get this new movie in. You see, every weekend they would bring in the latest movies that had just been released to DVDs. I had been anticipating this one movie, and when it arrived, I was one of the first to the TV room. So I was in the upper TV room when all hell broke out. The movie had just started and I was all the way into it, when the TV room door quickly opened and this guy screamed out that it was going down outside.

At first I thought he was just playing, but when I looked out the TV room window, I saw guys rushing to every window leading to the outside. This was confirmation that something major was going down.

I also rushed to see what was happening, but when I got to the window there were so many already standing there that I couldn't see. so I quickly grabbed a chair and stood on top to see. And what I saw was unbelievable. It was a full-fledged riot going down, and the two parties involved were easy to recognize even from this distance. To the north of the institution stood a massive group of black inmates, and to the west stood a massive group of Mexican inmates both armed with broomsticks, mopstick, and whatever else they could get their hands on. The only weapon neither side had was that of any type of prison shanks, at least not visible to the eye. Without any warning, the black inmates would rush the Mexican group, and they would exchange blows for a few minutes before rushing back to their neutral positions. This event looked so much like an action clip out of the movie, *Braveheart*. With every exchange of blows, blood was shed by both sides, but mostly by the Mexican side. Yet it wasn't because of the lack of trying.

Truth be told, the majority of black inmates just was more skillful when it came to the art of fighting. Yes, there was a few Mexican inmates that was holding their own, but they too were overtaken by the more advanced black inmate fighters that quickly recognized their skill level and welcomed the challenge. The attacking went on for what seem like hours. The quietness of the unit caused chills to go up my spine. When I looked to see what was happening. I saw a group of black inmates going to the doors of every Mexican inmate that was still in the unit. Moments later, the remaining Mexican inmates was at the unit door asking the unit officer that was standing guard outside of the door to let them out. When the officer asked why, they all said because they feared for their lives.

I knew that not one of those Mexican inmates that were left inside were involved. So when one of my close friends that was a part of that group came toward me, I asked him why did they do that, and his response was simple. Until they knew exactly what was going on, they wanted to make sure that we were totally safe inside the unit, so the separation was necessary really for both parties. The magnitude of inmates involved placed the officers that were present in harm's way, so they quickly sent out a distress call to all surrounding institutions, and within minutes, officers from here, the low and the camp was dress in full riot gear, armed with tear gas, and bean bag rifles. It took a full-fledged assault by the officers in riot gear to regain control. The inmates quickly realized that they were no match, nor were they prepared to withstand the tear gas and bean bag attack by the officers.

The Officers had gained full control of the riot, at the same time only a small number of inmates from both sides were placed in special housing. Truth be told, it was simply too many inmates involved to be locked up, so they only grabbed only the ones that they were able to recognize. We were all placed on lockdown until a full investigation had been conducted. We remained on lockdown for a good two weeks. To everyone's surprise, not one inmate from either side had to be hospitalized. Even though it was still popping in an F.C.I. Had this occurred in a U.S.P. there would have been body bags filled of inmates. We soon found out that all of this started behind a TV room that was assigned to the Mexican inmates. Yet being that no Mexican inmate was watching their TV, a couple of black inmates decided to go inside there to watch a movie. When one of the Mexican inmates saw them in there, instead of asking them to leave, he demanded them to do so, and from there things escalated. Make no mistake about it. Prison is prison, and it's still popping in an F.C.I.

CHAPTER 30

Finding Your Place

With so many opportunities, I'm not sure what I'm going to do here at this institution. Since arriving here, all I'm feeling is a great sense of peace, even after witnessing that riot, what most would have viewed as a major catastrophe. I'm still not use to this type of atmosphere. It's so different here that finding my own place is a little hard to do. I kept myself busy in the U.S.P. to stay out of the way. But here there's nothing in your way. I wanted to go back into Unicor, but I wanted to take some time to really enjoy myself and this peace. Yet you have to have a job, so I decided to work in the unit as an orderly.

Hey, everything is good. I have a cool cellmate, and now I have a simple unit orderly job. I'm really finding my place here. The only downside to this place is all the complaining some of these guys do. Now that gets on my nerves. You've got these guys that has only been doing time for a year with only two or three more years to do, crying about that simple little time, when I've been down twelve years with no sight of freedom on my side, not to mention the places I've done those twelve years.

When I get tired of them complaining, I simply tell them about some of the murders I've seen, and how men are turned into playing like women. Boy, you should have seen their faces when I was telling them those stories, you could actually hear a pen drop when I stop talking. Every one of them were looking like they saw a ghost or heard a ghost story. At times I feel as though every inmate should go to the U.S.P. for a while, and then I thought no because most of them wouldn't make it out of there. Anyway, I'm just focus on finding my place here. Things are truly moving along. The compound was rapidly getting full and still, besides that riot, it was as peaceful as ever. Boy, if you had to do time this was the place to do it. Don't get it twisted, there were still fighting, but they used their hands instead of a knife. This was still prison, and I still had that life sentence, so all of this talk about being in a better place is just because of where I've been.

Believe me, there's no substitution for freedom and being with your loved ones. Hey, it's plenty of guys here that view this place like being in hell especially those that were here to witness that riot. And whom am I to say they are wrong? You have to understand I'm speaking from what I've experienced, and I'm certain that they would feel the same way if they were to go where I've been. At the same time, they all understand where I've been and just where I'm coming from, and they do not want to experience that degree of imprisonment. To be honest, I also understand their point of views, as well as their reasons for complaining. A week in prison is too long, no matter where you are. So I get it. We all have to find our own place.

As was expected, George W. Bush was reelected January 2005 by defeating the Democratic Party's candidate John Kerry, the then junior senator from Massachusetts. So we all prepared for more of the same, at least I did. Some of the hopeful inmates were praying that he would do more for us on his way out being that he had nothing to lose now. Mind you, it's only a few more days left before 2006 rolls in and there's been no changes as of yet. So like I've said. I'm not holding my breath, for one thing that Bush had been all on top of since the 9/11 incident, has been the war on terrorism.

Being that I'm a unit orderly now, I have lots of free time, and I would really like to farther my skills level. I've worked ten years in Unicor, and I received the highest of honors while working there. So I can show a good work ethic, but I have nothing to show when it comes to academic achievements. Therefore, I will focus most of my free time achieving some of those academics. I'm already taking a Spanish course, and I'm just about finished. So I'm planning to start the second Spanish course next month because I really enjoyed the first Spanish course. Then I plan on enrolling in some Wellness Programs because I have to keep my body strong and in shape. This will allow my mind to think better. A healthier body, a healthier mind. Finding my own way here isn't always that simple, but at least my chances of becoming a victim here in an F.C.I. wasn't as high.

CHAPTER 31

Hidden Treasure

Just a couple of years ago in 2004, this young black senator named Barack Obama delivered the Keynote Address at the Democratic Convention at a packed Boston Convention Centre, becoming only the third African American to deliver such a speech at a major political party convention. Before this speech, very few of us knew anything about him. Even after that speech, he still remained what I call a hidden treasure. Yet to most of us inmates that heard that speech, he was viewed as a much-needed breath of fresh air. I can recall listening to that speech, and all I heard and saw was an intelligent black man with charisma. His style was unique. He spoke in a way that was so appealing to the ear that everyone had no choice but to listen. He left you wanting to hear more. What I found to be even more surprising is that he delivered this speech without sounding like a black preacher. Yet preach in an unusual way he did.

The young black senator wasn't the only hidden treasure that would be discovered. My Wellness course had just started, so I was all into getting the body right. At the same time, I wanted to go to the educational department and check on a few academic courses they had to offer. I had been told that most of them had already started, so I would have to wait until the next registration date. But I still wanted to know more about them. I was totally amazed by all the major academic courses they had to offer. It went from a drafting course, to an HVAC Certification course that came with a lifetime license. Then they had a Custodial Maintenance course and a Restaurant Management course. I truly didn't know they had all of those hidden treasures at our disposal.

Like I said, I could always show a good work ethic. Now when I do obtain all of those academic achievements, there's no way I will be denied whenever the time comes when I'm given my opportunity at freedom. You see, believe it or not, one that is serving time is judged by their achievements while serving that time. Inmates are pushed to do more to prove they are worthy of a second or third chance. Though the system is designed for one to fail, they do give you the opportunity to succeed. They even push you in that direction. I will start off just taking the drafting course, then I will move forward. Time is truly moving on, and I can't thank God enough for keeping me focus and safe.

After seeing all of these academic courses, I could see that light that led to my freedom even more clearer. At the same time, to obtain all of these academic courses, it will take some time, and being all I had was time, I didn't see any problems with a life sentence.

I knew I had to do more, show more, and become more than a regular inmate to prove myself. These hidden treasures would give me the opportunity to do just that. So many years have passed, so many loved ones have gone to that other side. And I'm still fighting to be free. I'm only human, how much more of this fighting can I take? I guess I can take as much as possible in order to regain my freedom.

Even from my hell, I see many reasons to keep on lighting. Yes, there are times I want to give up and just accept what is. But then I see my mother and her hopes of her baby boy coming home one day. I've disappointed my mother a lot during my lifetime, but this is one time I won't let her down. She is truly my greatest hidden treasure.

CHAPTER 32

Life without Love

When I was first given this life sentence, I accepted the fact that I would have to do life without the women of my past. I knew it wouldn't be fair to ask any woman to do this time with me when I had no date. Especially considering the way I was when I was a free man. Like I said earlier, it wasn't like I was Mr. Faithful. Matter of fact, I was totally the opposite. I was considered by most as a lady's man and that's putting it lightly. At the time of my arrest, I was juggling five different relationships, and numerous of side chicks. Even though a few of those relationship were with my kids' mothers, it still didn't make it right.

I can honestly say that such behavior also contributed to my downfall. Anyway, even though I cut ties with all the females that were in my life at the time of my sentencing, I'm still a man with a desire to be loved. So from day one, I have reached out in hope of finding not really love, but at least a female to converse with for as long as possible. I knew that with a life sentence, most women wouldn't be staying around long, so I got used to them coming and going just as fast. Back in 1993, the only means of reaching a lady's heart was done by a pen pal system. You had different companies that had pen pal list for sale, and I had no problem paying for those list. I will be honest I got plenty of pen pals and those many conversations really helped me do this time in an atmosphere that was designed for you to fail.

For a little extra, we could also be placed on the pen pal list for women to see us. So you know I had to do that as well. A lot of my friends would ask me how was I able to capture so many women's hearts. First of all, I told them that you have to be honest and let the woman know just how much time you had because they have the right to know. He went on to ask me how did the women accept you having a life sentence. Well, it's easy for me to share my life sentence because I never really accepted it, so when I told women about my life sentences, I did it with so much passion they really had a hard time with not accepting my person. You see, I had a saying I used to share with the ladies that stopped by for more than a minute. I would say to them, "Even though my body remains in bondage, my ability to reach out to one's heart remains as free as the birds that you see within the sky."

I would go on to say that I come to bring the purest form of joy to one's heart. My main goal was to gain one's trust because so many from here has truly placed a black eye on the hearts of many good women that was willing to look beyond one's present state of condition. At the same time, I wasn't willing to accept the blame that came from someone other than myself. I only desired to be judged by my own actions. Let me earn your distrust before you give it to me so freely. Even with a life sentence, life without love was not an option. My writing skills as well as my talking skills led me to many conversations. Even with a life sentence, I stayed with a positive attitude and in turn, I passed that attitude to the hearts of many.

But at the end of the day, when you're serving a life sentence, no matter how positive you are, no matter how sweet you are, no matter how loved you have become, that life sentence has its way of running that love away. I had grown to accept that fact, and when the time came for me to let one go, I always did so in a very respectful way with no hard feelings. Even though at times I had grown close to that person, I never had a problem saying goodbye because I truly felt that they deserved to be loved by someone that could show them that type of love face to face.

So many years have passed, but it hasn't been one year I have gone without the presence of women's company. Yes, many have come and gone, and yes, they will continue to do just that for as long as this life sentence is a part of my life. Yet when it's all said and done, life without love or a companion is never an option even with this life sentence.

CHAPTER 33

When the Getting Is Good

I was just eighteen days away from completing my Wellness/ Nutrition course when this junior United States senator from Illinois announced his candidacy for the presidency on or about February 10, 2007. Even though he wasn't the first black man to run for president, every one of us that heard his speech knew for once in our lifetime it was a strong possibility he could actually go the distance. Not saying he would actually win, but at least it sounds like he will be giving them all a run for their money. I'm telling you that when the getting is good, there's nothing that can bring a person's spirit down. I knew it was a total long shot for this young senator. But hey, nothing is impossible. God knows I would have *never* thought I would be serving a life sentence for such a simple charge, yet here I am today doing just that.

My mother thought me to think things into existence, to claim it right then and there. So I'm claiming the doubt-ful. That's one of the main reasons I've decided to prepare myself for freedom by obtaining all kinds of academic achievements. With all of these many possibilities on the arisings, there should be no type of hesitations on my part. My mission became even more clearer, obtain those academic achievement, and prepare myself for freedom. When the getting is good, it always has a way of getting even better. I was on my way to register for the Drafting course when I overheard two inmates talking about some kind of petition. On a normal day, I wouldn't have been eavesdropping, but when I heard these two inmates talking about some kind of petition, one could file to the president for a sentence reduction, I was all ears open. I had no choice but to intervene.

I quickly said, "Excuse me. So sorry for the interruption, but I had to ask you guys more about this petition to the president that I overheard the two of you talking about." They both where just as eager to tell me about it. The first inmate to speak said that this petition has been available to all inmates for years, but you have to ask your unit team for the paperwork. The paperwork is a petition for commutation of sentence that goes directly to the president. When I asked them why haven't I ever heard about such a petition, they simply said that it's just something our unit team doesn't tell no one about because he guess it would be extra work on their part, especially if every inmate decides to file this petition.

Hey, I had filed numerous of motions, and they all had been denied, so I knew I would be giving this a go as well. I couldn't wait to obtain this petition. So I went directly to my case worker and asked for this commutation petition. You should have seen the look on her face when I asked her about it. At first she tried to act like she didn't know what I was talking about. So I explained more about the petition to her.

When I told her it was to the president, I could tell a green light went off in her head. She then knew exactly what I was talking about. But it took her awhile to find it, and even then it was like the only copy, so she made me a copy. I couldn't wait to get back to my cell to really give it a good look over.

It was a six-page petition to the President of the United States. It started off by saying "The undersigned petitioner, a Federal prisoner, pray for commutation of sentence and in support thereof states as follows…" I was totally blown away after going over this petition.

I was even more upset about these people keeping such vital information away from us. At the same time, I wanted to be totally prepared when I did file this petition. I knew I was already headed in the right direction by wanting to obtain all of these academic achievements, and I wasn't about to change those plans. All I could think about was the possibility of that young black senator becoming president. At the same time, I still knew that I had to do everything in my powers to earn the right to be free, no matter who became president.

I knew it would take me a few years to accomplish my goals, so I had to be patient. For once in a long time, I really had something to look forward to even though it was a long shot, it still was enough to keep me headed in the right direction. I'm telling you when the getting is good, the bad doesn't have a chance. Six months later, I was enrolled in a Drafting course. Oh, how time flies and to everyone's surprise, it's been a relative quiet six-month journey around here. Not nothing more than a few fist fights from time to time. Like I said, when the getting is good, wrong is far gone.

CHAPTER 34

When Faith Is Lost

I continue to hold on to faith because faith is *all* I've got. Yes, there are moments when I just want to give up but when you're fighting this kind of battle, you're doing it with so many others in your heart. To let go is to let down *all* of those who love you dearly. And they are the ones that are depending on you to do *all* you can to get back home to them. Yes, when faith is lost, the pain with that lost goes way beyond these prison walls. It has a major effect on everyone that loves you. And in such an atmosphere, when faith is lost, there's just no telling what else is to follow.

Take it from a man with firsthand experience. There was this guy that knew a good friend of mine that had recently got out. The guy would always stop me to ask me about our friend, being that he knew we were close and we always stayed in touch. Our friend that got out was doing good out there. When I told the guy this, he would always get the biggest smile. I went on to tell him about the work our friend was doing out there, which was truck driving. The guy really got excited because that was the same trade he was taking up. Matter of fact, that was a course he knew my friend had took here, and he was in the same class now, so that was a very good sign for him.

He walked away from me with the biggest smile ever. At least once every other week, he would stop me to ask about our friend. He would also tell me about how good he was doing in the trucking course. I would always tell him to keep up the good work. So often when you're doing time, it makes doing that time somewhat better when you hear about the success of a former inmate, especially if you knew them personally. Matter of fact, you really didn't have to know them personally to share the joys of their success. It just gave you hope and it keeps your faith strong when you heard good things about a former inmate. At the same time when faith is lost, whether you're a free man or an inmate, there's no telling where you will end up.

Sometimes freedom can be your worst nightmare. This was truly the case for this one inmate that went home. He was a very quiet guy that got along with everyone. I just knew when the day came for him to go home, he won't be coming back. He had a sweet girl and daughter that visited him often, so he had a very solid foundation to go home to. He was a local guy from a city nearby. Anyway, one morning I was headed to do my orderly duties when I saw everyone standing in front of the TV. When I asked one of the guys standing there what was going on. He asked me did I remember T. I said yes, the quiet guy. Yeah him, he went on to say that he just killed a police officer, and they killed him.

This brought me chills, and I was really shocked by this news. All of this took place in his apartment bathroom. The officers were attempting to execute a search warrant when the first officer to enter the bathroom was shot and pronounced dead hours later. The end of that gun fire exchange also left T dead. When faith is lost, no matter if you're free or incarcerated, there's just no telling what will become of you.

It was chow time and on my way to eat. I saw my new friend the truck driver, which was the nickname I gave him being that I really never asked him his real name. Again he had that big smile on his face, as he asked me about our friend the real truck driver. I told him that he was on the road headed across state. I also told him what my friend the truck driver wanted to tell him and that was to keep up the good work and that there were plenty of driving companies looking for CDL drivers. This news really got him all excited, and he vowed to finish the trucking course. He went on to say that his sentence was about up after so many years, and he couldn't wait to be free and driving trucks.

A week had passed and I hadn't seen my friend the truck driver. I always looked forward to seeing that big Kool-aide smile of his. Another week went by, and I still hadn't seen him. I knew his unit so I was planning on stopping by tomorrow to check on him. Later on in the early part of the next morning, deuces went off (deuces is when all staff members' radio goes off simultaneously with a distress call). I was awoken by all the commotion but had no idea what was happening. Later that morning during breakfast, everyone was talking about this guy that hung himself last night. When I asked them who was the guy, one of my friend told me it was that guy that I'm always talking to. Of course I didn't know who he was talking about being that I often talk to many guys. But when he said the one with that big smile, I automatically knew just who he was referring too. At the same time, I really didn't want to believe it.

I just kept asking why would he do such a thing. It would be a week later before I found out the answer to that question. It was said that he had been indicted for a murder that happened years ago in his hometown. So I guess he simply lost *all* faith and decided that he would rather be dead than to do even more time. At the same time who really knows what would have been the outcome of that trump up murder charge had he chose to fight it? Yet when faith is lost, so is the spirit to fight against its known cause.

CHAPTER 35

Historical Moments

I just completed my Drafting course, and I passed it with flying colors. I'm not the only one passing things with flying colors. Listen. I never would have thought that this young senator out of Illinois would be making this kind of noise. I'm really beginning to think this young black man can take it all the way to the White House. He already has a leg up on the two key Democratic runners (Hillary Clinton and John Edwards). He's constantly making historical moments. And to be honest, he's doing it without making racial conversations. The man is stating facts on top of facts.

The buzz around here is louder than I have ever heard it. I mean from inmates to the staff members, this young Illinois senator, is the talk of the compound. We haven't missed not one of his speeches. Like I said I'm not sure what the future holds for this senators. I'm just overly excited about the possibility. I'm not the only one wanting to see history being made. I'm sure every African American on this planet want to see this happen for the first time ever. I mean who wouldn't want to see one of their own race accomplish this unbelievable achievement known to mankind. An achievement that has never been accomplish by an African American. Could this really happen? Could we actually see the first African president in office during our lifetime?

Every inmate around here began to reach out to their family members to push them out to vote, and this started something even bigger. For the message reach to every Federal institution and every inmate was sending out that same message. Could we have an effect on the outcome? Only time will tell. But I do know this much, a lot of our family members had never voted, yet they all were on their way to the polls for the very first time. Because they wanted to see their loved ones home, and we told them that we believe if elected he would be doing just that. He even spoke of those things, he spoke of a change that was coming. He also spoke of the overcrowdings and the unfairness of the sentencing process. To every inmate doing time, all that he said sounded like a man that was going to make some much needed changes throughout the prison system and the world.

The thought of this happening is truly unthinkable. But the possibility of this happening would move way beyond a historical moment. It came down to Democratic Party Hillary Clinton and Obama. On June 7, 2008, Clinton made a formal announcement to end her candidacy. She then endorsed Obama and made it clear with a passionate declaration. With every step this Illinois senator took was a step into history.

With an excellent team put together, Obama set records with his ability to secure contributions and funding at a record-breaking pace. His ability to use the Internet as a marketing tool was brilliant and was also one of his many historical moments. On August 23, 2008, Obama would announce Senator Joe Biden as his vice-presidential running mate. On August 27, 2008, Obama was nominated by the Democratic Party to run for President of the United States of America. Making this another historical moment. There would be high and low moments for this young senator, and for all of us that shared our full support, but on November 4, 2008, the dreams of the majority were realized. With fifty-three percent of the popular vote in his favor and 365 Electoral College votes, Senator Barack Obama won the election over John McCain and became the first African American to be elected President of the United States of America. On January 20, 2009, he was sworn in.

Screams of joy could be heard throughout this whole prison compound when that announcement was made. As I witnessed this moment, it only confirmed the fact that *nothing* is impossible. Not only was it the ultimate motivational tool, it supplies me and so many with an unbelievable amount of faith. I just wished that my grandmother, and so many others, could have lived to see these many historical moments being made. If you're wondering if the efforts of so many inmates reaching out to their family members made any kind of difference with the outcome of this election. Their own statistics say it did.

I was even more determined to continue my quest for freedom. I had no doubts when it came to giving this life sentence back. I knew that once I had achieved all of these academic achievements I had set for myself, there would be nothing standing in my way of freedom. I enrolled into not one but two academic courses, doing them both at the same time (Custodial Maintenance Apprenticeship, and Restaurant Management Course). Yes, I knew this would present a huge challenge for myself, but after seeing the first African American being elected president and seeing all of those historical moments being made, I myself felt invincible.

CHAPTER 36

Living in the Moment

Change truly has come, and I'm living in the moment. Yes, I'm still living in my hell, but after all I've witnessed, I know even more changes are about to come. It doesn't even feel the same around here. It just feels more peaceful and guys seems to be in better moods. Some are still walking around in disbelief. Of course no one here truly knows what the outcome will be with our first African American president, but everyone is very optimistic. Time is really moving fast and I'm beginning to regret taking on two academic courses at the same time. The Restaurant Management course is very challenging within itself. But there's no turning back now. I can only do my very best.

You know the thing about living in the moment here, at the drop of a dime all hell can break out and snap you right back to reality. That was the case today. You have to understand that not everyone around here like the fact that a black man was elected into the White House. Especially certain gang members that happened to be affiliated with one of white gangs. So on this particular night, this one white inmate got drunk and started to get out of line with some innocent black inmates that were just trying to watch TV. They tried their best to ignore him, and they went as far as to go to his cellmate for his assist with his celly.

They then went to all the white inmates in the unit, in hope of them helping solve the problem before it got out of hand. Yet this one white inmate manage to break away from them all. He then ran right up to the first black inmate in sight and swung on him. I guess enough was enough, and within seconds all hell broke out. Not only did that black inmate aggressively attack that one drunk inmate, the other black inmates joined in an full force retaliating against any white inmate insight of the fight. Because they blamed all of them for not putting that one white guy in his cell. Of course, with all of the commotion, the unit officer quickly hit the deuces (the distress call to all officers). It took a few minutes before they all arrived, and the meantime, some butts were being kicked royally.

It was no need for me to intervene because those inmates that were involved were handling their business to the fullest. Yet I was forced to intervene mentally because when I look down over the rails of the second floor, I saw one of my good friend just whaling away with this chair to the face of that one drunk inmate repeatedly, I was so afraid he had killed him because the guy wasn't moving or nothing, so I quickly screamed out to my friend, "Boy, stop. Stop." And it was like my screams snapped him back to his senses, and he stopped immediately.

Soon after he stopped, the officers rushed into the unit and placed the whole unit on lockdown. But before I went in my cell, I was watching to see if that one drunk inmate that started all of this was moving, and for the longest he didn't move at all. but then I saw a twitch of his head, and I was a little relief mainly because I didn't want to see no one die for such a small matter. Yet the only thing that save him was the fact that the chair my friend was using to beat him was made of semihard plastic. Had it been made of metal or even wood, the boy would have been dead.

I was quickly reminded that living in the moment here isn't the time to drop your guards because in a blink of an eye, all hell can drop by. We stayed on lockdown for a few days after that altercation, then everything went back to normal. After a while, all the hype just went away. No major changes had been made, at least none that effected doing all this time. I had little time to think about all of the happenings because I was at the completion of one of my two courses. I passed my Custodial Maintenance Apprenticeship with flying colors.

Yet my Restaurant Management test wouldn't be going as smoothly, matter of fact, a few days later I found out that I failed the test by two points. I was very disappointed, especially after I was told that if I wanted to retake the test, I would have to pay to do so. Hey, I wasn't the only one to fail, but I was the only one that really cared about getting my Restaurant license. Even though your unit team would automatically give you an E for effort, and you would receive high participation points. Some would have happily accept that much recognition. But that just wasn't good enough for me, and I was determined to do whatever it took to obtain my Restaurant license, including paying the forty-five dollars to retake the test. So I studied a little harder, which was easy to do this time around being that I didn't have to worry about the Custodial Maintenance Course.

The next time I took the test I passed it, thank you, God, and I was overly proud of myself and my ability to keep focus after failure. Living in the moment this time was surely something I created through persistency and a pure desire to succeed.

CHAPTER 37

My Hail Mary Pass

I've been that modest inmate for years now, from the day I entered the prison system in 1993 to this year of 2010. Against all odds, I've managed to stay above water, within the most horrific environments. I've been moved across the country without a voice to refuse. I've witness countless acts of catastrophes. I've lost appeals after appeals and at this moment this life sentence holds almost every part of me in captivity. Yet there still remains a part of me that has been very elusive and refuse to be captured. My faith has been my shield of protection. Even without a date, my faith has kept me strong, focus, as well as determined, to overcome.

Seventeen long years have passed, and so many changes have transpired. My kids are no longer babies; they are young adults now. So many family members as well as close friends are no longer among the living, and even my goodbyes remain in captivity. My mind is engulfed by a million thoughts of regrets, desires, and concerns. And it is constantly challenged by insanity. The weight of two worlds leans heavy on my shoulders, yet suicide is never an option, even though the ghost of its very being haunts me on a daily basis. Even the strongest of mind-set is tested. No one is exempt.

I've cried many nights in silent for so many years without being notice, not even once. I've prayed every prayer known to mankind. There's been so many low moments in my life that I'm afraid that I won't be able to recognize a high when it comes my way. At the moment, I'm a fighter with no wins. Yet I refuse to give up or give in. Not continuing to fight is not an option, even when you see no sight of victory. I've done everything I could possible do to help my chances of victory. I've prepared myself mentally and physically. Now the time has come for me to throw my Hail Mary Pass. (A Hail Mary Pass is a very long forward pass in American Football made in desperation with only a small chance of success).

My Hail Mary Pass will come in the form of a Commutation Petition to the President of the United States. To be honest, it was only a short time ago that I even knew such a petition existed. Not to mention out of the seventeen years I've now served, I have never even heard of such a petition being granted. So my chances are truly slim to none. Yet it is that of my faith that keeps my hope alive. With a nothing-to-lose attitude, I begin to take a deep step back knowing it's going to take all I've got to launch my Hail Mary Pass. I can't afford to get professional legal help in this matter and I truly believe it's not really necessary to do so. First of all, I've got the best legal assistance in God Almighty, and second of all, who knows your situation better than one's self. So with God's true guidance, I will file my own Commutation Petition to the president.

Even though it's a six-page petition, I can see that it will take some time to prepare. I've waited this long, so a little longer will not be a problem. My main focus point is making sure that I put my *all* into this petition because I truly believe this will be my Hail Mary Pass that will get me the freedom I've been preparing to receive. I've been very excited about the possibility. I've even told many others about this petition and they too knew little about it, at the same time none of them showed the least interest. They all seem to feel like this would be a waste of time. But me, I see it as a hidden blessing, so none of their negativities has strayed me from my mission.

A commutation petition to the president gives the president the right to substitute a less severe punishment in place of the punishment originally imposed. A sentence may be commuted when facts become known that were not known at the time of sentencing, or that came to light and were developed after. Commutation is rarely granted but can occur in cases of old age, illness, and when the sentence is unusually harsh compared with similar cases. I myself will base my whole petition on the last stated fact, "When the sentence is unusually harsh compared with similar cases."

It's truly been a long time coming, and yet I believe that this is my hidden blessing coming to life. Therefore, I will do my part by throwing my Hail Mary Pass. Yes, I know my chances remain slim to none, yet I'm willing to take this chance. Because I would rather fail trying than to just sit here waiting for something to happen on its own. Matter of fact I've been doing that, and I'm still in this same position. As I sit here preparing to launch my Hail Mary Pass, I say a silent prayer to God asking for the strength as well as the knowledge to finally overcome my hell.

CHAPTER 38

Believe Me Not

My main focus at the moment has been preparing this Commutation Petition to the president and I've been overly excited about the outcome. But no one seems to share my enthusiasm. At least no one around here. My family members on the other hand are just as excited about the possibility. My kids' spirits are not as strong because their spirits have been let down so many times that they view my enthusiasm like the boy that cried wolf. They've heard my enthusiasm so many years, when it came to my freedom, without any results, that they are so tired of being let down, they just have a harder time believe in that possibility now. Yet believe me not for I myself believe that if I continue to do what is right, I shall overcome. If I continue to hold on to faith, it will be that faith that brings me home. Believe or believe me not will not hinder me from trying.

I've tried everything else, so I have to believe that this could be that blessing that has been so elusive for so many years. Again I will be the first one to admit that this is truly a long shot, some around here would consider the odds similar to the chances of one hitting a 200-million-dollar lottery. Yet it's the chance I must take. So believe me not. Just sit back and watch me shoot my shot or should I have said throw my Hail Mary Pass. A lot of guys around here is still hoping our first African American president will simply open these doors for us. But it's almost been two years that has passed since he's been in office and nothing has changed when it comes to sentencing reform. A lot of us are still carrying the burden of an unbelievable amount of time.

With all the negative vibes I've been receiving here of lately, concerning this Commutation Petition, I knew that there would be one person that would believe in the impossible, and that would be my mother, from day one she's been my rock of positivity. She's never wavered from the belief that one day, I shall be coming home. When any kind of doubts comes my way. I can always count on her to put those doubts in their place. No one has stood so firmly by my side during these trying times. Even after seventeen long hard years, my mother remains the pillar of my foundation. So many have come and gone, yet her presence of devotion and commitment is as strong as the day I was born into this world. Could it be because I'm the last one she bared? Maybe that's part of the reason, but surely her love is just as devoted, as well as committed to both my siblings.

Speaking of my siblings, they too share my belief that this could be my opportunity to freedom. So when all those negative vibes come my way, I turn to the ones that share my beliefs. Believe me not is never a part of their thoughts. I feel so blessed to have such a supporting family. For so many around me aren't as fortunate. As I look back into time, I see moments of fear, confusion, desperation, as well as determination. I see the full transformation of the world. Technology has taken off like I've never seen before. And I yearn to experience its changes.

I've seen acts of war launched against those who have caused lives to be lost in America. I've seen acts of racism swore throughout what supposed to be the land of the free. I've seen Mother Nature lash out in a rage like no other throughout the world, although most disasters are surely man-made due to wars and terrorism. Yet the world has witnessed numerous disasters here of lately, just to name a few. There was Hurricane Katrina and Pakistan Earthquake in 2005. Then there was Cyclone Nargis in 2008 and just recently you had the Haiti Earthquake in 2010. Surely these natural disasters will go down as the worse ever to be recorded.

Trapped in my own nightmare for the last seventeen years, I've seen lives taken by others, as well as lives taken by selves. I've been so close to death that I now can recognize its scent. I can only hope that this will be the key that will unlock the door to freedom. So many prayers I've said, not only for myself, but for others as well, especially for my father that's been fighting that battle against cancer. You see my freedom quest isn't just about me. It's for those that need me home like my mother and father, my kids as well as my siblings. So believe me not is your right, but to believe is my only light through the darkness of my journey to freedom.

CHAPTER 39

When Hope Faces the Ultimate Tragedy

I'm at the ending of my Commutation Petition, and I'm very optimistic about its possibility. Everybody I've read it to had nothing but good things to say about it. One of my close friends we call MT told me after he read it that if there's any truth about this whole petition process, once they read your petition. I know you will be set free, there's not a doubt in my mind. MT went on to congratulate me on a petition well written. All of this positive feedback really lifted my spirits and I just knew the outcome would be just as great. I shared my petition with everyone I could get to listen or read it for themselves because I wanted to hear their opinion rather it was positive or negative. I was really surprised by all the positivity.

At the same time, no one was convinced enough to file their own petition. For the life of me. I just couldn't figure out why not. It cost you nothing but a little of your time, and the way I saw it, time was all we had. Believe me when I had finished my petition. I left no stone unturned. I wrote this petition with every part of me and my only helper was God's true guidance. I dotted every I's and crossed every t's.

I read it to my mother and father, and I told my father to hold on because I would be coming home soon. My hope was at an all-time high, and that hope spread like a wildfire. My spirits were unshakeable and no matter what was going on around here, none of it fazed me. My mission was so clear, and all I saw was my freedom.

This petition was based on hard facts, as well as the highest degree of honesty. It was full of emotions that demanded entrance into the reader's heart. Hope led by faith ensured me a clear path to freedom. My spirit were so strong that even my kids started to believe. I truly felt untouchable. As I was putting the finishing touch to my petition, I got word that my father had passed away today August 8, 2011. I just couldn't stop asking God why, my whole world seemed to crumble at that very moment. I've fallen time and time again, and with each fall I've discovered even more reasons to rise because sometimes the message you need to see lies beneath one's feet, therefore, in order to be able to see or even read that message, one has to fall to his or her lowest point.

But one is never judged by the falls, but it is the persistency of the rise that gets the full recognition. All my hopes were now facing the ultimate tragedy. At the last part of my petition, I included a P.S. which I stated: Mr. President, unfortunately my father passed away today 8-11-2011 before I was able to get this petition sent off. I went on to say that this is a very sad moment for me and my family. As I wrote those words, tears ran uncontrollably from my eyes.

Even though my petition was complete, it took me four days to get my petition in the mail. At the same time, I knew my father would want me to continue to fight, continue to believe, and by all means continue to hope even with the tragedy of his passing. But to lose someone that was totally responsible for your being felt like losing half of the body you now possess, it's like being physically cut in half. What finally gave me peace was the fact that my father knew how much he was loved by me, he knew that without a doubt. So often we take life for granted. Not knowing when God will call us home. So for those whose parents are still well and living, let your love for them be known, for tomorrow they could be gone. No matter what your differences may be. No matter what happened yesterday, don't let another moment pass without resolving whatever problem that causes you to stay away from your mother or father.

As I placed my petition in the mail, all I could think about was the last one standing, the last one just as important, and that was my mother. Even though I knew she knew how much I loved her, I couldn't wait to tell her again and again just how much more she's being love by me. You see, even when your hope faces its ultimate tragedy, there's never a reason to give up or to give in to any type of adversity. Take it from a man that has lost everything including seventeen years of his life. A man that still carries the burden of a life sentence, without any possibility of release, at least that's what they say. Me on the other hand, I know my day is on its way and when that day gets here. I'll be more than ready to succeed.

On the fifteenth of August 2011, my petition was respectfully submitted, now all I could do was wait for a decision. So I placed it all in God's hands and waited patiently on the outcome. I knew it might take some time being that next year would be reelection year. As it now stood, President Obama has pardoned more turkeys, than he had inmates, and just as few Commutation Petitions during the first three years of his presidency. At the same time this was a normal act of a newly elected president, during their first four-year term. Especially one that wanted to be reelected. So I prepared myself for next year's election before my petition would be denied or granted.

CHAPTER 40

A Second Time Around

On November 6, 2012, Obama was reelected for his second term as president, and everyone around here was just as happy. Even though he did very little for us during his first term, we just knew he would be doing way more on his second time around. At least that was one of our greatest hopes. With a nothing to lose attitude, we all knew we would be getting the type of president we helped get into office. Yes, a second time around is just what the doctor ordered. There were truly endless possibilities on the arisen. And just as I expected, there had been no decision made on my petition, and it has been over a year since it had been filed.

There had been so many changes happening around here. The first one happened on February 19, 2009, when inmates were allowed access to electronic messaging through e-mails. The message must be text only and must be conducted in a secure manner between inmates and the public. All messages are subject to monitoring. This really gave us all another great avenue when it came to reaching out to our loved ones. Because this avenue came with no limitations, as far as the amount of e-mails one was allowed to send out. None like the phone system were you were only allowed 300 minutes a month. This really allowed us to form a stronger bond with our kids and family members.

Then came the implementations of the MP3 players. Man, there's nothing like being able to pick and choose your favorite music. This was truly something that would serve as one of the purest forms when it came to obtaining inner peace. You know the saying concerning the effect of music it can soothe a wild beast. And believe me there's plenty wild beast throughout the prison system that will be effected by the presence of an MP3 player. I can only imagine the sincere effect it will have on everyone. When I first heard about the MP3 players coming, I thought it was just talk. I just couldn't believe they would do something like that. When it finally happened, they sold out within minutes. But not before I came up in line, yes, I was one of the first to get one on this compound. I can't begin to tell you the joy as well as the total comfort it brought me.

The cheapest songs would cost you over a dollar and some would cost more than two. So it was very costly but believe me it was worth every penny to me. When I listened to my MP3 player, it took me back home in the purest form. It kept me walking down memory lane. It also gave me the power to relive the most precious moments of my past. Even moments that I had forgotten all about. Every soul that had been lost during my many years of incarceration, I would find through the music. Everyone I loved and lost would come back to me in a certain song I played. I could smell the bacon and eggs cooking at the house my daddy would take us to in Belton, Texas, on a summer weekend, and in the background coming from my daddy's room. I could hear The Temptations singing "My Girl." I could hear my daddy humming that song. At that very moment, my heart felt my daddy's presence like no other. I saw my father in his purest of form and he would remain that way with every song that brought him back to me.

It was truly a family reunion with every song I choose, and everyone was invited. Both of my grandmother's would stop by on a regular, and my cousin Norris stopped by to remind me who taught me how to drive a stick. My cousin Big Junior, would stroll in my grandmother's house wearing all white making jokes, and my Aunt Hellen would always try not to show a smile. Granddaddy stopped by to make one of his best grilled cheese sandwiches, with the main ingredient being government cheese. A second time around was truly an understatement, when it came to the magical effect of music.

CHAPTER 41

A Love of One Kind

With the newest addition of your own chosen music, many thoughts of love entered my heart. Mostly from my past, for those were the most precious times of my memories. At the same time, I had let those feelings surpass years and years ago. But with all of this music, one couldn't help being taken back in the hands of time. You see, the music made me think and feel more. I mean it got me back in the mood for love. I've been so focus on filing this petition that I lost contact with the lady friends I had been talking to from time to time. With the ability to e-mail, that really gave me access to the world.

Anyway, I really didn't see any reason to reopen relationships I had allowed to close. So I decided to look into various dating sites. Of course, we aren't allowed direct access to any kind of dating site, but there were third party sites that would gladly play the middleman and get you registered on different dating sites and would be responsible of getting you any message from whomever as well as getting your message back to them.

With that being an option, I decided to go that route, so I had this third-party company to place my ad on a few dating site. Yes, I had them to place me on regular dating sites, and I also was on a Christian Dating site, as well as an Islamic Site. In the past, I have been very blessed to receive lots of responses, but with a life sentence, it's only a matter of time before that interest fade away. It's very hard to hold on to a woman's heart when both of your hands are chained together and locked by a key that no longer exist.

Yes, with many of those relationships a life of love came fast, and most of them would convince themselves that they could love beyond my life sentence, yet not truly understanding its ability to destroy even the strong will of commitment. Even with my full knowledge of understanding, even with me sharing that understanding with them, that served as a warning. They still insisted to be that one that can handle the weight of my love. Of course I knew better, nevertheless I would always give one the freedom to prove me wrong, after all how would I ever know if I didn't give one that chance?

Time and time, the end results were always the same. The only difference was the amount of time one would stay. Yes, some would stay around for weeks, some even a year or two, but eventually they all seem to fade away, and I never tried to stop them because I truly felt that they all deserved the type of love I just wasn't able to give. At the same time, I truly felt that a purpose was accomplished with each heart that I had encountered. After all, I was placed in here for a reason. And only God knows that which I don't. Yet that never stopped me from yearning a love of one kind.

I had always told myself that if I find that love of one kind I would settle down and marry that woman. Because I just didn't want to be the type of man I was when I was free. I experienced being that worldly man, now I wanted to be that good man with morals and principles. I wanted to do things God's way. I wanted to look for the inner beauty of a woman. I no longer was interested in one's outer appearance, for surely the heart supersedes the physical aspect of a person. Finding such a woman has proven to be easier said than done, for after seventeen long years I have yet to find her presence.

But that doesn't mean she does not exist. I take each step toward that possibility as if she's waiting right around the corner. I know one may be thinking why is it taking so long, and my answer to that question is the same reason it's taking just as long to regain my freedom. And I haven't given up on that, so why would I give up on a love of one kind? My search did start off very promising because within my first week or so I received lots of interesting responses but none that touched my heart in the way it desired to be touched. It was really more of the same. Women expressing their desire to find love, at the same time condemning such a love really exists. And all of this was based upon actions committed by the men of their past.

You see, so often we are judged by the actions of someone other than ourselves. And surely my present state of condition didn't help that chain of thought. A life sentence would only add to the negativity of that thought as well. I've learned from past experiences that it's hard to change one's way of thinking when the heart carries such a huge burden of pain. Even when that pain wasn't caused by you. Nevertheless, pain is pain, and no matter who caused it, the hurt is real and it can last for a long time.

To be honest, I could totally relate to their pain, for I've caused that same degree of pain to the hearts of many when I was a free man. A lot of women blame themselves and think it's something they did. That's when I would take it upon myself to let them know just how far from the truth their way of thinking could be. I gave it to them from a worldly man's point of view, and I told them how selfish we could be. How greed has led us astray. Even when a woman gives us their all, greed tells most of us that we need more. I explain to them that it's nothing they done. It's just the nature of most men to always want more than they really need. The sad thing about it all that most of the time, one has to lose the best thing he ever had, to truly realize how blessed he truly was.

When she finally arrived, she wore words that I had never heard before. As she was walking toward me, the stylish shoes she wore spelled out loving words of sincere concern. She walked through the door complimenting me for being that strong black man she saw beyond my present state of condition. She encouraged me to stay the way I appeared to be. As I read her words, all that came to my heart was a love of one kind. Could this really be her? With my mind lost in hope, I hadn't noticed the date her words were written. It was July 31, 2012, when I received her message, but she wrote that message on June 1, 2012. Almost two months ago. I was sure I had lost the chance to reply because of the time that had past. I had never received such a message so late, and I was really wondering how did it happen. Then I noticed the name of the site it had come from.

It was the Islamic Site. I then remembered cancelling that site for a while before being advised by the site provider to rejoin. So this was just one of the messages that was written to me when that site was cancelled, but now that it was reopened I was able to receive her message. Now I'm left to wonder, *Is it too late to reply?* Well, maybe or maybe not I just knew I had to try because if this is that love of one kind, she'll still be waiting on my response or not. When I sent her my reply, she really didn't remember just who I was. Matter of fact, she didn't even remember writing to me. As I was explaining to her what had happened and why I took so long to reply, it was like a light switch came on in her head and she remembered just who I was. From that moment, that love of one kind was as real as could be.

CHAPTER 42

Distant Lovers

I guess you could say that it was love at first words because our words never stopped coming to one another. Distant lovers were truly an understatement because our words brought us closer than close, and closer than most. A month had past, and we felt as though we've known of one another forever. The bond we had built in such a short period was unbelievable. It was all built in the purest of form. Especially from my end because after a month, I still had no idea how she looked physically, and I didn't care because I had fallen in love with the person she was. Yes, it was that of her inner beauty that had won my heart. Yet for her, she had the best of both worlds, because she did know how I looked because my site had pictures of me which she was allowed to see. That was one of the privileges I wasn't allowed.

Our vibe was strong, our connection was even stronger. I just knew this was that love of one kind. I told her everything about myself, and she fully accept me for me. At the same time not everyone shared her enthusiasm, her family and friends constantly questioned her decision.

They just wasn't comfortable with me being here and my life sentence really took their message to that next level. She was being pulled from every direction, and even the strongest of will can be pulled down when there's so many doubting the sincerity of our love. Being that I truly understood their reasons of concern, I was able to reassure her of my love. My ability to do that gave her the strength to rise beyond the words of others.

I not only told her about my petition to the president, I sent her a copy of that petition. I also informed her of the time it was sent and of the current statue of my petition. This gave her even more hope. At the same time, I wanted to be more than distant lovers. It's been almost two months now, and I just knew she's the woman I've been waiting for, so I didn't hesitate asking for her hand in marriage and she didn't hesitate accepting. She went on to ask me what I thought my mother would think, and at first I didn't understand the question. She then said, concerning my age. I then realized that I never even asked about her age nor had I even seen a picture of her. At the same time neither one of those things was a concern to me, but now I was curious to know her age. At the time, I was fifty years of age, and I automatically assumed she was around my age or younger.

She continued to ask: what I thought my mother would think with her being close to her age. That question kind of caught me off guard, so I had to ask how old was she, and she said sixty-two. Before her age registered in my mind, I simply answered her question by saying, "I'm sure that wouldn't be an issue with my mother being that the man she's with happen to be my age." We both laughed and the age difference never came up again. One week later, I received a few pictures of my queen, and just as expected, her outer beauty matched the inner beauty I fell in love with. On October 18, 2012, my marriage proposal was made official, for on that day her wedding ring set arrived.

I knew with this kind of commitment, I had to get closer to the woman I love because she deserved as much as I could give her and being distant lovers just didn't seem right. So I decided to put in for a transfer to Colorado. So we could at least be able to see one another on a regular basis. I knew it would be too costly for her to be traveling this far. Mississippi was a ways from Colorado. We talked about that transfer and she was all for it. I had been here for the last eight years, so I was really due for the change. I had accomplished all I could here, now it was time for me to go. Of course, this would take me even farther from my family, at the same time I was already too far from them. I hadn't received one visit from any of my family members since I've been here. So I was sure they would understand.

My transfer had been approved, and it would be only a short period of time before I would be on my way to Colorado. I was so excited, and so was my fiancée. Yet after eight years spent here, it was always hard saying goodbye to the people that's been like family for all these years. You can't help getting close to people when you're around them day in and day out for eight years straight. Even in my hell, there has been moments of happiness. I've experienced with my family here. Yes, I consider a lot of my friends here family and I love them just as much. So yes they all will be missed because they are my brothers. There's one thing they will never be and that is forgotten. Even if freedom comes my way. I will forever be there for them. If not by words, by spirit, I will always be in their presence. This will make my fourth journey into the unknown, and I pray it will be my last. There was one thing for certain, this journey will take me and my love from being distant lovers.

CHAPTER 43

Up and Away

Bye bye, Mississippi, and yes up up and away I go. I'm finally leaving and I'm ready to see the next chapter of my life. Yes, I'm headed to another FCI in Colorado. I've been told that it's a very laid-back place and I can't wait to get there. Though I'm going to another state, it's not like that state is a total stranger to me. Matter of fact, I have a lot of family members there as well. I have two uncles and two aunts plus lots of cousins there on my father's side. I've never been up there, but I've seen that part of my family numerous of times when they came down to Texas to visit. With my father gone, I was hoping to strengthen the bond with his siblings. So there were lots to look forward to.

Again I wasn't looking forward to my ride on the Ole Blue Bird (a Federal aircraft) with what has always looked like duct tape on the wings. I've gotten use to flying now, and the only way to go for me is up up and away. The schedule time of my arrival was a day before my birthday which will be April 25, and even though I wasn't one to celebrate a birthday, if I did, this would be considered a very good birthday gift. Yes, I'm on my way to see the love of my life. I can't thank God enough for the many blessings he has stored upon me. For the last twenty years, God has been a shield of protection over me. I mean I have yet to have one single fight, and beside my leg injury, I'm in the best shape of my life. Yes, even with a life sentence, I'm still blessed. God knows it could be worse. So always be thankful, no matter what life brings your way or no matter what life takes away.

The last two Federal institutions I helped open up and I stayed a total of sixteen years between the two. Now I was headed to a well-established institution that had been opened for years. My goal was simple: blend in and stay out the way. I was really excited because this would make my second F.C.I. and I was told by guys that had been there that it's much better than here. So I knew I had made the right decision. There's one thing I could never get use to when it came to flying under my current situation and that was being totally chained up from the waist on down. I think I'm a little paranoid after watching the 1993 remake movie, *The Fugitive*, the part of the movie that stuck in my mind was when the plane went down into a river and most of the inmates died because they were chained up and couldn't get loose.

At the same time, there was nothing I could do about that, so I simply tried my best to keep that movie scene off of my mind. To my surprise, the Ole Blue Bird had been replaced with a newer version. There was no sighting of duct tape anywhere. I guess after so many years, it was time for an upgrade, and I was very happy about that. As I board the new Blue Bird, I couldn't help thinking about the last eight years spent in Mississippi, in my first F.C.I. An F.C.I. I helped open. I had to admit, beside a few moments of drama, it was a very peaceful stay, compared to those twelve years spent in two of the worse USPs. Yes, I was blessed to make it out of those two places. At the same time, I still carried the burden of a life sentence, that same life sentence that will be joining me when I arrive in the state of Colorado.

I can't begin to explain the total weight of a life sentence. Just knowing that of its full meaning, I'm talking about doing so many years, without a date. Where hope seem hopeless. If I was given a 25-year sentence at least I would know when I'm to be released. Not knowing is truly another degree of punishment and can also be viewed as a crime within itself. How I've managed to stay sane for the last twenty years can *only* be the work of *God himself.* Truth be told, I would have given up totally years ago. But what appeared to be a life sentence, was only part of my life's mission. You see, the lives I've touch during the last twenty years is a confirmation of a planned mission. The fact that I have yet to have one physical altercation in twenty years is another confirmation from God. Just for being who I am have saved lives. My cooking ability has given comfort to so many for so many years. My words of encouragement reaches beyond the prison walls that has confined me.

As I look back, I see me then as I was a stranger to me now. How could I have been him? How could I've been so naïve? How could I've made so many bad choices? Yet had I not been him. there's no way I could have become me today. With my mind so entwined, I hadn't noticed the takeoff until the Blue bird ascended above the clouds. I felt so close to God at that moment. All I could do was praise him for bringing me so far. As the plane landed in the state of Colorado, all I could think about was my newfound love. I couldn't wait to let her know that I had arrived.

It was a short bus ride to my new F.C.I. and when I finally got processed, it was time for me to go to my new unit. As I was walking across the compound, the mountain view was breathtaking. I had never seen nothing like this, it was like I could reach out and touch them. The air was fresh and the sky was clear. The scenery was simply unbelievable. I was so at peace just by that view. As I walked into my new unit. I felt very comfortable.

I was then place into my assigned room with my new cellmates. It was too late to call my baby, so I simply went to bed knowing that not only will I get to call my girl in the morning, it would also be my birthday. I will be turning the big fifty. So many years beyond the age of twenty-nine when I first arrived within these conditions, and all I can do is praise God for bringing me safely to this day. For tomorrow is promised to no one. But God himself has blessed me with twenty years of tomorrows.

CHAPTER 44

Mountain Time

Not only am I in a new state, I'm also in a new time zone. Meaning I have to now wait an extra hour before my birthday. Had I still been in Mississippi or even Texas, it would have already come, being that it's now five minutes after eleven. Now I'm on mountain time in Florence, Colorado. I'm now only a couple of hours away from my baby. I can't wait to tell her I'm here. I will be doing that first thing in the morning. It's so beautiful here, and I just can't get over the mountain view. I have always heard about the altitude, and the way it can affect people that's not use to it, so I'm wondering what effect, if any, will it have on me, so far I can't tell any difference.

This makes my fourth institution, and I'm praying it will be my last. It's been over a year now and I still haven't heard anything about my petition to the president, but the way I see it, no news is good news, meaning at least I haven't been denied. Well it's official, my fiftieth birthday has arrived. And I have to thank God for the many blessings he has bestowed upon me, and the many more to come. Like I've always said it would have been so easy to just give up

172

but to have done so would have went against everything I truly believe. Even after all I've been through, all I've seen, I still have faith. I do believe my day will come, but it will only do so when God sees fit. We have to truly understand that God's time isn't the same as ours. His second can be like an hour. His hour can be like a day, his day can be like a month and his month can be like a year. And I'm only guessing at best.

It's been a very long trip, so I better get me some rest. The morning couldn't get here fast enough, so when I was awaken by the breakfast announcement, instead of heading that way after I washed up, I headed to make my first call to my fiancée. It really sounded good calling my girl that. I was already planning to make it official in our first visit. I had to do it the proper way when the time was right. You see, getting down on the one knee is a must. I'm not sure if that's allowed, but hey, this is one time I'm just going to do it. When I finally made the call, my baby was overly happy to hear the news about me being here. Now the next step was getting my visitation papers in so we could meet face to face for the very first time. She had already been approved on my visitation list when I was in Mississippi, but here I had to do it all over again. I was really hoping everything would go just as smooth here as it did there.

After talking to my baby, I went straight to my new unit team to request a visitation form. As I was filling the form out. I got to the question where they asked you did you know the person prior to your incarceration? Though this question may seem to be rather innocent, it has been proven to be far from that. I learned this the hard way.

When I was in Terre Haute, Indiana, I was introduce to a lady that was a friend of an inmate there, and she wanted to visit me. So I requested a visitation form, and when I got to that question about knowing her prior to my incarceration, I told the truth and said no.

For that reason and that reason alone, the visitation request was denied. I never got to meet the young lady. After that experience, I only had two choices when it came to meeting new people, either I stretched the truth, or I would never get to meet someone I never knew. With a life sentence, there's just no way I could deny the opportunity to meet new people, when I knew I had no one left from my past. Other than my family members of course.

Well, I will admit that during the course of time. I've had many visits with women I've never known, and unfortunately the truth had to be stretched in order for those visit to happen. But with my fiancée, I told the truth when I was in Mississippi, and my unit team understood, and they approved my visitation request. I know you may be asking yourself why take that type of chance, especially with this being a very serious relationship. It's for that exact reason, because of this being a very serious relationship I wanted to make sure everything was done the correct way, even if the outcome would have been different. At the same time with that being said, I was already prepared to fight to make sure I saw my baby when the time was right. But thank God I didn't have to go that far. Would the outcome be the same this time around. I really didn't know, but I would be telling the truth once again.

It took only a week before I was told that my visitation request had been denied. I was crushed by this news, and I knew my baby would be even more crushed when I told her. And she was. She was so hurt with this news, that she started to cry. She really couldn't understand why they would deny our visit, especially after all we've been through getting close to one another. I quickly reassured her that I will *not* accept their decision, and I will fight them with all I've got to make sure I see my baby.

When I hung up that phone, I went straight to the warden during chow time and explained to her what had happened, and she stuck to policy and told me that the reason behind the denial was totally correct and that she stood behind that decision. I quickly assured her that I would not be letting this go and that I would fight her decision as long as I'm here. I went on to explain to her that she was my fiancée and not some lady I'm just trying to visit, and that she's the only reason why I'm here.

The warden listened but she still stuck to her guns, and I did the same. As I walked away, all I could hear was the crying voice of my baby, and I was even more determined to fight. The next day, I was right back in front of the warden, and this time I came with my visitation papers from Mississippi showing my fiancée being approved. When she saw this paper work, I saw a change in her approach. She then asked me did they know about the two of us not knowing of one another before my incarceration? I said yes. She then asked to keep the paperwork so she could get verification of these facts. Even after verification, I still remained in limbo. Months passed and there was still no resolution. Yet I stayed persistent, and I never wavered. Last week when I saw her, she straight out asked me, you're not going to let this go. And I simply told her that I just couldn't.

On July 1, 2013, when I saw the warden instead of me having to stand in line to see her. She called me to the front and told me that she's decided to give me and my fiancée a special visit on the twentieth of this month, just to see how it goes. She went on to say that this is only a trial visit and nothing more. I was so happy by this news I didn't care what kind of visit it was just as long as I got to see my baby. I rushed back to the unit to call my girl, and she was to happy, and I told her that I wouldn't stop fighting until it happened. So the next couple of weeks we spent getting ready for our first visit. She had already informed me that her oldest daughter would be driving her down. She had always told me that if I could somehow win her oldest over, that would be half if not all the battle.

I have to admit, that her oldest was a tough nut to crack. When we first talked, she was like a drill sergeant that didn't bite her tongue and spoke her mind. She also didn't have a problem letting me know heads would roll if her mother was to ever get hurt, and the head she was speaking of was mine. She didn't mind showing how overly protected she was when it came to her mother. At the same time, if I continue to make her mother happy, we would get along just fine, and I assured that would be the outcome of this relationship as long as I'm in mountain time.

CHAPTER 45

Picture-Perfect

It was truly a picture-perfect moment when I first laid eyes on my fiancée. She was everything I envision her to be and even more. The joy I saw as I approached her truly equaled that of my own heart. As I reached and grabbed her left hand, the engagement ring I brought her she wore proudly. I seemed to stubble into her arms, as my lips made their way to hers. A lingering kiss presumed thereafter, taking us both to the brink of ecstasy. Had there been any doubts on either one of our part, surely those doubts have been replaced with the purest form of happiness. Hours wore the clothing of minutes, as time went as fast as it came. We sat among many as if many weren't even there. For the first time in years, I felt totally free. Everything I had lost I found during this very special visit.

I wanted so badly to hold on to this moment, and when my thoughts were interrupted by the announcement of picture taking time, I knew this would help me hold on to this moment. Plus it would give me the opportunity to make this official. So my first pose was on one knee asking for her hand in marriage, and without hesitation she said yes. She had worn the wedding ring set up here, and that made the moment even more real. A picture-perfect moment was truly an understatement, for this was one of the best moments of my life. It was a very strong connection right from the moment we saw one another in person.

Everything felt natural, it didn't feel like this was our first time meeting one another, it was as if we had known of one another forever. We kissed and hugged, we talked and laughed, we ate and we took pictures. We did all of these things as a loving couple, and my present state of condition had no say so, even the life sentence was powerless. This was truly a day when God himself showed who was really in charge. The hours went by like minutes, and before either one of us knew, it was time to say goodbye. I really didn't want the visit to end but that was something I had no control over. Our first kiss was simple and sweet, but our last kiss or should I have said kisses, were sensuous and lingering to say the least. As we parted ways, our eyes never deviated away from one another. Though no words were exchanged, the eyes themselves shared their own love story.

Yes, I did have to fight for this picture-perfect moment, and I must say it was truly worth the fight. Every visit thereafter was truly that picture-perfect moment, and they gave me even more reasons to continue fighting for my freedom. Her presence brought back an even stronger desire to succeed, as well as a more determined will to overcome. At this very moment I felt like there was nothing I couldn't overcome. My faith was at an all-time high, and I just knew my life was headed in the right direction. For the last twenty years I had prepared myself for freedom, and I allowed nothing to stand in my way. Would all of my efforts, all of my patience, soon pay off? I guess only time will tell.

With every visit we gained more than before, and our love grew stronger and stronger. Yet my prayers remained the same, continuing to ask God for my freedom. Sometimes after my prayer, I would get this indescribable feeling of happiness. I just knew it was God's way of showing me that he heard me loud and clear. It's been over two years since I filed my petition to the president, and I have yet to be denied. So that has to be a good sign from God. At the moment, I'm just enjoying the love of my life and continuing to prepare myself mentally and physically for freedom. You see, if you don't prepare for the unknown, the unknown take it upon itself to prepare nothing for you in return. If you just see the negative part of prison life, you stop seeing what life really has to offer you.

Prison doesn't have to represent the ending, especially when it offers so many different opportunities to succeed. If you've never worked a day in your life, prison gives you the chance to learn how to become a productive worker. If you didn't finish school, prison gives you the opportunity to do just that. If you fail to go to college, prison gives you the opportunity to gain that degree. If you lack a trade or a skill, prison offers you the chance to learn one of your choice. Yes, it's so easy to make excuses, to place blame, or to just go with the negative flow. To be a man, one has to understand as well as recognize when it's time to make that stand. You see, when freedom finally comes my way, I will have earned every part of it.

Well, it's now official, the warden has removed the special visitation title, and I'm now allowed full visitation rights with my baby. So we are totally happy about that. Like I said, every visit is truly a picture-perfect moment. We've become closer than close and even her family and friends now share in our happiness. Gaining her oldest daughter's approval really helped set the tone. But we all know only time will tell the real story. In the meantime, I will just continue loving my baby to the fullest and making each moment we shared picture-prefect.

CHAPTER 46

When Will My Prayer Be Answered?

It's been twenty long years now and I'm just sitting here thinking when will my prayer be answered? More than two decades have passed me by. The loss of loved ones has made me cry. I've lived in the midst of chaos and confusion, madness mixed with murder, self-destruction mixed with suicide for the first twelve years of this life sentence, yet I managed to keep my sanity throughout those years. The eight years that followed wasn't as bad but wasn't good either. Because no matter where I laid my head, I was constantly reminded that of my imprisonment which carried the title of a life sentence. It didn't matter how much I've accomplished or how behaved I was. That title never changed. For the last twenty years, I was no less off than a murderer, or a terrorist. Matter of fact, I was worse off than either one of the two for the most part because at least most of them had an out date.

I can't even begin to describe the emotional roller-coaster ride I've experienced for the last twenty years. I claim to be sane, but is it more insane to be making that kind of claim? Surely every claim remain an assumption at least until I experience freedom. It would be so naive of me to believe I will know the world as it is twenty years later, when it's totally different. I came from the beeper era. Now twenty years later, I still have yet to touch a cell phone. The speed limit was fifty-five when I was out there, now it's seventy-five. And it's been twenty years since I've been behind a stirring wheel. Only God knows how these two changes will affect me, not to mention the many other changes that has come to pass within the last twenty years.

With all of that said, still twenty years later I'm asking when will my prayer be answered? My faith is constantly being challenged, and though I remain undefeated, I still face fear of the fact that the life sentence I've carried for so many years comes with no answer. Truth be told, if I was to look at my situation through the eyes of so many others, I would see no hope. The loss of hope can easily lead to the loss of faith and without faith the will to overcome is truly lost, leaving one totally vulnerable. As you can see, even when you manage to find a reason to smile, prison or life, reality has its own way of making you cry or sad. Patience is truly your only shield of protection when it comes to waiting for your prayer to be answered. Believe me, God does hear us *all*.

When you're thinking otherwise, that's *only* the devil doing what he was placed on this earth to do, lead us astray. Just take this moment for example, it's a beautiful day out and I'm sitting out here in the rec yard enjoying the beautiful mountain view. Even though I'm still in a prison atmosphere, it happens to be a very peaceful day. To add to that is how blessed I am to have found the love of my life. So when it's all said and done, I'm still being blessed. At the same time, one has to remember even at your happiest moments the devil always has a way of spoiling that moment, but he has no control over the rest of your life. So keep holding on tight to your faith and surely God will answer all of your prayers. And I mean when you least expected.

Well, I'm on my way back to the unit from the rec yard because it's almost lunch time. I'm looking forward to lunch because it's Wednesday Fried Chicken Day, my favorite. The only bad news is that my unit happens to be eating last because meal time release order is determined by a weekly unit cleaning standard, and this week, our unit came in last place, so that means we will go to all three meal calls last. There's a total of eight units so that will be a long wait. When it comes to the food here, it's really not all that to look forward to. But on Fried Chicken Day, that's a different story. That's one meal everyone looks forward to. Truth be told, it's almost impossible to mess up fried chicken, even though at times they do, but for the most part, it's always worth coming to get.

In the meantime, I'm getting my clothes ready for my next visit, which will be coming next weekend. In five more days will make my eighth month being in the State of Colorado. In for the most part, it's been a very peaceful stay. It did start off a little tough, with my visitation rights with my baby, but it's all good now. So I'm really feeling blessed. I was sitting back watching TV when I heard my name being called from the PA System. I was being summoned to the lieutenant's office. My first reaction was concern because everyone knew there could only be two reason to be summoned to the lieutenant's office, one was to receive an incident report, meaning a rule had been violated by your person, or two, you were chosen randomly to take a urine drug test. Being that I knew I hadn't violated any rules, I was sure it had to be a random urine drug test, which I had no problem taking.

There was one thought that really made me smile and that was the fact that I will be among the first group going to lunch. With that thought on my mind, I rushed to the lieutenant's office. To my surprise upon entering the lieutenant's office, after giving him my name, I was told it had been a mistake and I wasn't the one they were trying to call. I didn't hesitate making my way out of there. I could see they had called the first unit to lunch, so I quickly made my way up there. The aroma of fried chicken filled the air and I was already plotting my chicken heist. Now I will admit I'm not one to break any kind of rules and trying to get two pieces of that fried chicken was breaking one of those rules, at the same time the punishment if caught is truly worth the risk, the worse outcome is a little extra duty, which would most likely be picking up trash around the compound.

At the same time, this wouldn't be my first attempt when it came to the fried chicken heist. Believe me, I had a platinum move that hadn't been caught yet. All I had to do was keep my eyes on the one kitchen officer that was trying to watch both lines. As the line server which happened to be an inmate placed my piece of chicken on my tray, I quickly moved it underneath my tray in lightning speed without hesitation. I knew the kitchen officer didn't see the move, at the same time the inmate was hesitant to place another piece on my tray because he knew he had already given me one. Regardless of that fact, he also knew the consequences that could come to play if he was to assume the role of a prison officer. The look I gave him assured him that I was also totally aware of those consequences of his actions, so without further hesitation, he nonchalantly placed that second piece of chicken on my tray, I returned a smirk and quickly walked away.

As I approached the table I will be sitting at, all I could see was naked chicken bones flying to the side. I couldn't wait to join the chicken massacre. I quickly removed the hot sauce from my pocket and after saying a short grace, I started in on that juicy piece of chicken, just as expected this was one of the times they got it totally right. I was savoring every bite of my first piece of chicken and had already made plans to take my second piece back for a late-night snack. I was all lost in the moment when I heard my name being called by a familiar voice. It was my cellmate. Our unit had just made it to the chow hall, and while in line my cellmate called to let me know that they were calling me to go to the lieutenant's office. My response was: I've already been up there. His reply was: Well they are still calling for you. At that moment, I saw the lieutenant that told me it wasn't me that they wanted. So I decided to go back to him to make sure that fact remained the same.

When I approached him, before I could get my words out, he informed me that it was me that they needed to see, and I should go right back down there. I then asked him could I go finish my lunch first, and he insisted that I go now. So I beckoned to one of my friends to watch my tray, and his nod let me know he would. I rushed back down to the lieutenant's office, gave my name, and was told to go wait on the bench that was right outside the office. As I was waiting, all I could think about was that good fried chicken and I couldn't wait to go back to finish. As I was sitting out there, the warden and a couple of her associates were approaching, the warden quickly said, "That's not a good look you sitting out in front of the lieutenant's office." I quickly told her that I can assure her that I've done nothing, and she replied I hope not. She then turned to go inside the lieutenant's office.

As I continued to wait outside the lieutenant's office, all I could think about was getting back to the chow hall. My chain of thought was interrupted by my prayer being answered, yes, I was finally being called into the lieutenant's office, so that means that there was a good chance of me making it back to chow in time. When I walked into the lieutenant's office, the first person I noticed was the warden sitting at the lieutenant's desk and her two associates standing to the side of her. I found this to be odd but I really gave it no major thought. The warden welcomed me in and seated me in the chair in front of the desk. The lieutenant stood at the right side of me. I wasn't sure what was up but whatever it was, they needed to hurry it up because my chicken was getting cold.

The warden started off her conversation with this topic concerning inmates getting together with the outside community to build this casket for a little girl that passed away recently. She went on to say how special that moment was.

Now I don't mean to sound inconsiderate or heartless, but all of this small talk wasn't getting me closer to the chow hall. I did manage to show interest and the purest form of concern. The warden went on to say how outstanding my behavior has been since my arrival here, and she had my personal files with her to back her point. Which she happily displayed them to her two associates. At this point I didn't have a clue where this was leading up to.

Again my thoughts were interrupted when the warden stated to me, "It happened, Mr. Wheelock." I was totally lost with that statement, so I quickly asked her what has happened. She went on to say that the president has granted me executive clemency. My heart stopped beating, and my mind went blank, as she started reading the executive clemency order that went as followed "To All To Whom These Presents Shall Come." Greeting. At this point, my whole body went numb and my ears went deaf. I could only see her lips moving but I heard nothing, with no control, tears fell rapidly. At the same time. I was in totally disbelief and totally shocked. Question after question invaded my mind, could this be true, am I dreaming, did she say the President, after all of these years, is my prayer finally being answered? With my heart starting to beat a 100 miles an hour, tears continue to fall uncontrollably, every part of my body shaking wildly.

Trying my best to regain my composure yet totally trapped in twenty years of hoping and waiting on this moment. Lost beyond lost not knowing what thought will come next. Fighting from falling down on both knees to give God all due praise. Yet constantly praising him with every part of me that can speak. What felt like an hour, was only minutes has passed since being told of this long-awaited blessing. As my eyes began to gain back sight, and my ears began to hear tones of life, the first realization of me regaining my composure came in the form of a hand full of Kleenex being given to me. Once I wiped my eyes and gently blew my nose, I could finally see the people before me and beside me. My eyes found their way to the eyes of a very compassionate warden and her peers. With the most heartfelt voice, she asked me was I all right, I tried to say yes, but I could only nod my head.

It took me another five minutes before I was able to talk. Even then it was only short answers and questions. Everything was so emotional for me. So I didn't or couldn't say much. I did manage to ask her when did she say I would be released, and she said in April. I just knew she wasn't talking about this upcoming April. Matter of fact, I didn't care which April she was referring to. All that mattered to me was that I now have a date. For the last twenty years, all I had was faith, faith without a date. At the same time, she assured me that it was April of the upcoming year, which would be April of 2014. The news really hit the very core of my heart. As far as I was concern, I was totally free at this very moment. Yet I would remain in total shock for days or even years to come. What seemed like a million thoughts ran wildly throughout my mind, before one could gain understanding, one hundred more screamed out for answers.

Before I made my exit, the warden informed me that I will be leaving her institution very soon because once my life sentence was taken away, my custody level was instantly dropped. The thought of my life sentence being taken away felt so unbelievable for it was a part of my being for the last twenty years. Even though it was the maximum burden for all of these years, letting go I found it to be just as challenging mentally. As I was headed back to the unit. I did so as a totally different person. What I saw going to the lieutenant's office, I didn't see coming back. Even the mountain view was new to me. I kept pinching myself to make sure this wasn't a dream, yet if it was I vowed not to ever wake up. Every thought known to me came all at once, but it was one thought was instantly lost and that was anything to do with a piece of fried chicken.

My life changed forever the moment I was told that I was granted executive clemency by President Barack Obama. As I looked back toward the lieutenant's office, I saw me just a while ago walking there with a life sentence, a life sentence I've been carrying for the last twenty years. When I turned my head forward, it was as if I was floating toward that so elusive freedom, that now stood still just waiting on my arrival. I no longer had to ask when my prayer will be answered, for today, December 19, 2013, God himself made his answer loud and clear.

CHAPTER 47

Praising God

As I was approaching my unit, all I could do was praise God. For his blessing came when I was least expecting. I mean, it had been more than two years now and I hadn't heard a single word concerning my petition to the president. So this news caught me totally off guard. I still can't believe it's real. I also can't stop praising my God. When I finally arrived at my unit, my cellmate was waiting right at the entrance door, there were other guys standing there as well because they were waiting for the next open movement to the rec yard. These open movements took place at the end of each hour.

The first thing my cellmate asked me was, what did the lieutenant want? Being that there was so many other guys around, I just told him it was only a random urine drug testing. I then walked to my room and quickly place a do not disturb sign on the small window on my door and fell straight on my knees praising God. With every word uttered, tears of joy, and disbelief ran uncontrollably. Especially when I thought about what this news would do for my mother, my oldest sister, my oldest brother, my kids, as well as the rest of my family members. Yet the main person was my mother, who have been my rock of all rocks, every day of my twenty-year journey. She never gave up hope and she never left my side. No matter how far apart we were, the presents of her motherly love was always nearby.

When my spirits were down, her motherly love lifted them back up. When I had little to no strength, her motherly love carried me where I needed to go. When there was no love of my life, there was my mother's love that never wavered, not even to rest at night. My mother's love was on call 24-7, 365 days a year, for the last twenty years, and not once was I unable to reach her. My superhero was and still is my mother. That same degree of love was also demonstrate by my oldest sister, Rosie and my oldest brother, Eddie. There wasn't a single conversation with either one of them that didn't end with, "I can't wait for you to come home." The both of them uttered those words nonstop for the last twenty years. So there's not a doubt in my mind when they hear about this news, they too will fall on their knees and give all praise to God. Chills traveled down my arms when I thought about them finally hearing about my long-awaited freedom.

I could have stayed on my knees praising God for days, without wanting or needing to take a single break. But I knew my cellmate would need his cell time as well, so I quickly got up and removed the sign from the door window, and only a few seconds went by before my cellmate made his way in. I guess he didn't believe the story I told him about the urine drug testing because the first thing he asked after entering the cell is what did the lieutenant really want with me. I then told him the real reason, and all he could do was give me the biggest embracement. This news caught him totally off guard, at the same time he knew it was more than a urine testing because he said the look on my face automatically told him so. He went on to say it was a look he had never seen. And I'm pretty sure it was.

Both of us sat there in total disbelief, not knowing what to do next. I'm just sitting there looking into my locker, just wondering what am I going to do with twenty years of accumulated property. Of course I would be leaving most of my property with my cellmate being that I knew he had a few more years to do. Again I just couldn't believe I would be getting out this coming April. While all of these thoughts raced through my mind. I heard my name being called again over the PA System and again I was being summoned back to the lieutenant's office. Me and my cellmate looked at one another, with the same puzzled facial expression. What could they want now I thought as I made my way back down there.

As I was walking in the direction of the lieutenant's office, I notice the warden and the rest of them from earlier waiting on the outside of the office. When I reached them, the warden quickly informed me that I will be leaving in the morning. When I asked her where will I be going, she simply said, I would know the answer to that question in the morning. She went on to say to make sure I'm packed and ready to go early in the morning. She also wanted to know if I needed to be placed in a cell by myself until then, and I told her no, I would be okay staying in my cell. She then told me how happy she was for me and wish me the very best in the near future. I thanked her, and I headed back to my unit. This time I was prepared to share my good news with everyone. As I entered my unit, I could see the curious glare that came from every eye that was looking my way. This was to be expected being that I had been summoned to the lieutenant's office more than one time today.

When I shared my good news with everyone in my unit, it was as if I became an instant prison spokesperson. Everyone was totally excited and just as happy. This news spread like a wild fire throughout the whole compound. My cell filled with inmates wanting to know how I did it. I told everyone. I would be leaving in the early part of the morning, and I knew I would be gone before anyone was up. So I said my goodbyes and I let them all know that even with my freedom, I will continue to fight this battle until the cocaine disparity is equal. The call for lockdown has now been announced, and some of the guys are still trying to ask questions. Finally, everyone has left our cell, this gave me and my cellmate time to say our goodbyes. At that time, I started to pack. I had a few pairs of tennis shoes, and all kind of clothing. I knew I wouldn't be needing all of these things, so I left most of my stuff with my cellmate and my lil cousin.

By the time I had finished packing, they were calling for me to leave. I hadn't gone to sleep, neither had my cellmate. We said our final goodbyes, praising God as we parted ways. I was now on my way to my next destination, where that may be was still a mystery to me. With every step I took, praising God was all I could do. I hadn't shared my blessing with any of my loved ones, and I couldn't wait to do so. I plan on telling everyone as soon as I got where I was going. When I got down to the transferring department, I was told that I would be going across the street to the camp. Wow, I've heard nothing but good things about camps. I'm still praising God with every step I took toward my long-awaited journey into the light of freedom.

CHAPTER 48

Lost in a Sea of Thoughts

Lost in a sea of thoughts as I made my way through the door of my first camp. To my surprise, there wasn't a single fence nowhere in sight. That really made me feel even more free. As I made my way to my assigned unit which happened to be like an open dorm style, it was like all eyes were on me. It was as if everyone knew I had just been granted executive clemency by the president. Seconds later, I was approached by this inmate, and the first thing he asked me was, am I one of the guys that just been granted executive clemency? I said yes and then I asked him how did he know, that's when I heard something I had no knowledge of. He told me that it's been on the news all morning worldwide. I then repeated worldwide, and he said yes. He went on to say that the media is referring me as being one of the Obama Eights. Lost in a sea of thoughts, I began to wonder if my mother heard or my sister and brother, or even my kids. What about my brothers in Yazoo, Mississippi, Beaumont, Texas, or even in Terre Haute, Indiana?

I really thought I was the only one that knew, now I am told this is worldwide news. I couldn't wait to call my mother to see if she had heard, so once I put my things away I headed straight to the phone. The excitement I heard from the voice of my mother told me that she already heard. She confirmed that fact with her next few words, "Baby, I got the newspaper early this morning and the first thing I saw on the front page is the news about President Obama granting my baby executive clemency, and that you would be coming home in April." She went on to say that, "I wasn't trying to get too excited because I didn't want to give myself a heart attack. At the same time, I knew God would be sending my baby home. Because I asked him to please let me see my baby out here before anything happens to me. Because God I love my baby so much, and you have to send him home to me." She went on to say that she knew he would be sending me home, just didn't know when. Even though twenty years has passed, her spirit and faith in that prayer remained totally convinced.

Mother told me that her cousin Angie called her around 7:00 a.m. this morning, which she found to be odd because she never calls that early. With the same news and she was overly excited, my mother's only response was, "Isn't God good." Once she finished talking to Angie, she called my sister and told her. All my sister could do was to rejoice with tears of happiness. My brother found out from his ex-wife, but he just couldn't accept it from her. So he called our mother and when she told him it was true, he was just as happy. It was like this huge burden was lifted off the shoulders of us all. I could just feel my mother's total relief and her happiness now soared beyond the stars. This news brought about a change, that I'm sure will last for the rest of our lives. When I hung up the phone, I was totally lost in a sea of thoughts, and I keep pinching myself to make sure this wasn't a good dream.

I tried calling my fiancée, then I remembered that she had to work all day. My mind still engulfed with this unbelievable news of freedom. I just didn't know what to do with myself. Being that I hadn't went to sleep. I thought I would try to do just that. When my head hit my pillow, instead of being able to sleep, flashes of my twenty-year journey ran wildly throughout my mind, and there's no way I would be able to fall asleep. Then these words came to my mind, so I had to get up and go straight to the computer where we had emailing access, and I began to type the following:

"The Thoughts of a Pardoned Man." As I sit here. I am consumed by a sea of thoughts. Some are of waves of joy and happiness, and some are of sorrow and regret. I can't thank God enough for the blessing of relief. Yet I can't stop hearing the screams of those who are no longer on this earth that didn't make it out of here, and of those who are still fighting for their right to be free. Yes, I have every reason to be happy, I also have even more reasons to be sad. I'm reminded of that fact, when those screams visit my heart. I wish I could share these screams with the president, with congress, and with the world, for if everyone could hear those screams, they would know what true pain and suffering is all about, of course that's if their minds are strong enough to withstand the unbelievable tone that comes from so many screaming souls. Though I will soon be free, it won't come without an even bigger responsibility and commitment. You see, my blessing came with many sacrifices, for you see, just two weeks ago, a dear friend was murdered in his sleep in Pollock USP, and it is that of his screams I hear the loudest, for he never made it out of this hell. He too had spent more than two decades inside these walls. Therefore, I can never be totally free, until I share with the world all that is within me, and even then, when day becomes night, who knows what scream will visit with me. I dare you to listen and I double dare you not to believe. These words caused several tears to fall, and for once in my twenty-year stay, it really didn't matter who may have been looking.

No, I wasn't pardoned by the president, but at this time, that word simply fits this message. After getting those words off my chest, I felt even more relieved. I was still trying to call my fiancée but still there was no answer. I couldn't help wondering if she heard about this news. My now grown kids, what will this news do for them? After so many let downs, so many lost holidays and birthdays, so many years without their father. Will they scream, holler, or cry? Only God knows that answer.

I'm just so glad for them because I know, no, I don't know, I really couldn't know that of their true pain and suffering during the absence of their father's presence. I can't even imagine the many lies they were forced to tell to protect their self-image when it came to questions concerning their father's whereabouts. So many years has past and as I look back into the hands of time, I see the many effects caused by my absence, and though I cannot change the past. I will do my very best to make a difference in each of my adult kid's life.

When I finally caught up with the love of my life, she couldn't believe what I was telling her. The first thing out of her mouth was, "Stop playing with me, Baby." Once she realized what I was saying was true, she was overtaken by the purest form of joy. I'm sure a sea of thoughts was running wildly within the very depths of her mind. How could it not be, when only seconds before my call, the man she was loving had a life sentence that carried no date. No answer when it came to when he would be free. Now out of nowhere, came a date and the answer. Being that we now had a date, the only thing left was to start the wedding process and that she did. After talking to her three phone call sessions in a row, with each call being fifteen minutes long, which added up to be forty-five minutes, we knew we better ease up. Being that we only had 255 minutes left for the month and believe me, those minutes go as fast as you get them.

As we said our goodbyes, I could feel her relief, as well as her joys. I had made a promise to myself years ago that whoever is left standing by my side when all of this is over, she will be the woman I would marry. Now I was looking forward to making my baby my wife.

CHAPTER 49

Into the Light

From the time I was given this life sentence, through the twenty years living with that sentence, finally instead of looking day in and day out for that light that will lead me to freedom. I was truly on my way into the light. Yes, that light to freedom was as bright as ever. And everything within that light was filled with joy and happiness. Not one conceivable thought caused me to be concerned when it came to living in the land of the free. Matter of fact, no matter what was in store for me, could never compare to the hell I lived in for the last twenty years. Surely every moment hereafter will be like a heavenly journey.

This feeling I've been experiencing since the moment I was told this news had totally reformed me in every possible way. Even though I still remain within prison confinement, I felt as free as ever. Not only can I see into the light, there's so many moments when the light appears to be so bright that it blinds me at times. So many thoughts continue to invade my mind, so many words I yearn to express to ears I've been denied to enter for so long, so many faces my eyes have been hidden from, so many voices my own ears have yet to hear. I came into this darkness, a father of young children. Now I enter into the light a grandfather of many.

With the year-end quickly approaching, all that I now see is freedom. Still lost in total disbelief, still trying to plan for a freedom I know nothing about. You see, preparing for something is nothing like experiencing. Especially when more than two decade has passed you by. How will I really live, when I've been denied to exist for so many years? Lost in a million random thoughts, all of a sudden I was brought back to reality by a knock on the entrance of my two-man cubicle. When I turned to see who this person was, to my surprise it was my case worker. She informed me that I was approved for the halfway house in Denver, and I would be leaving in the near future.

Though I was totally excited by this news, I truly wasn't looking forward to yet a million more new random thought that was surely on its way. The New Year came in with a *bang*, and my emotions were overwhelming, all I could do was to thank God, and I did so with a prayer like no other. Tears of joy ran uncontrollably. I just couldn't believe I've made it to this moment. God knows it's been one hell of a journey, and there's no way I could have made it without him. There's so many others that didn't make it. And I'm not just talking about prison inmates. It's been so many lives lost right out there in the so-called land of the free. I truly don't know what to expect, when I've been away for so long. Especially when there's so many missing from the only life I knew of at that time.

Here I am lost in the midst of a million random thought, when I heard a loud voice over the prison intercom instructing every inmate back to their units, the voice went on to say that we are officially on lockdown. Soon after I was told by another inmate that there was a full-fledged race riot going down in the recreation area. All I could think of was, *A race riot here at a camp?* The thought of such an act took me right back inside to the hell I had just left.

All I could think about was the well-being of those who were involved and that of their safety. I just knew there would be lost casualties on both sides. Yet after all the smoke was cleared, not only was there not one casualty lost, all the injuries was minor. Again I was reminded how blessed I was to be here. I'm pretty sure I was the only one feeling this way because most of the inmates here had never experienced a higher prison level than this. Because had they been a part of such bad conditions, surely they would appreciate the security that comes with being in a camp environment.

Nevertheless, this incident was treated as if we were in a very hostile environment. We stayed on lockdown for more than three days. You see, even though I was at the lowest level of imprisonment, you're always reminded that you're *never* truly out of harm's way, at least as long as you're in any kind of prison setting.

To be honest, I had let all my guards down, but they were back up and I mean in full force. Of course I continued to look into the light, but my peripheral vision stayed in full alert. Before I knew it, I was on my way to the Federal halfway house in Denver. I will never forget this day February 18, 2014, I was as nervous as ever but just as happy and excited. A long time coming was truly an understatement. When I was told to pack out, I did so in record pace. I quickly said my goodbyes, and out the door I went. That day came so quick I was unable to get clothes in to wear out of here, so I had to wear what the Fed's had available, and I didn't care. To my surprise, their clothes wasn't all that bad. A pair of jeans and a pullover shirt. Being that it was a little cool out, I also was given a life jacket.

I thought I looked pretty good on my way out. I was given just enough for a bus ticket and food. As I was pulling away from that prison life I've been living in for the last twenty and something years, all I could do was thank God. This was all very new to me, and I didn't have a clue of what to expect next, so I sat there in the purest form of amazement as I was being transported to the Grey Hound Bus Station. With only my prison ID and a prepaid credit card, I entered the bus station. For the first time in twenty years, I felt invisible as I walk up to purchase my bus ticket to Denver. Freedom truly came in many disguises, the first one I noticed was the ability to blend in. At this very moment I was an equal among many, yet I carried no known title. I received greetings from many as I walk my own way. I felt as free as the next man that continued to pass me by. For the first time in many years, I was seen, but not noticed.

Being that I would be making it to Denver a couple of hours before I had to officially check into the halfway house, I found the nearest phone and called my baby. Of course she had no problem meeting me at the bus station. She also added, that she would be bringing me my favorite food—fried chicken. The chicken sounded great, but as much as I love me some chicken, I wanted nothing more than to hold her in my arms as a free man. Especially being that I hadn't seen her since I was granted executive clemency. You see, once she knew of my date, she saw no reason to come visit me inside such a place. Quiet as it's kept, she never like seeing me there, but she was willing to make that sacrifice for as long as it took for me to regain my freedom, even if it took a lifetime.

As I took my seat on the bus, all I could do was smile like a big kid. I really didn't know how to act. I was observing everything around me. I felt like a kid at his first amusement park. After being around grown men for all those years, what I found to be absolutely captivating was the sight of little kids and babies. They looked like little human toys and watching them brought me so much joy as well as a little sadness being that I was denied the right to see the growth of my own. So many lost moments I will never get back. Yet I was totally looking forward to the many more moments to come. Before I realized it, the bus was pulling into the station.

I quickly grabbed my belongings and off the bus I went, not really knowing where to go. I simply followed the people in front of me. I just knew my baby would be nearby, but after searching the whole area, that wasn't the case. Of course anxiousness began to get the best of me, but before it got too out of hand, I saw my baby walking through the door, and my heart began to race. I couldn't make it over to her fast enough, and when we embraced, the weight of the world appeared to fall off my shoulders.

A lingering kiss followed which caused my heart to flutter with pure delight.

I couldn't begin to describe what she might have been feeling, but if it was anything close to what I myself was feeling, this moment was just as exciting and overwhelming for her own heart as well. Our embracement seemed to last forever, and letting her go was even more challenging. Still having some free time, we decided to stop by the home she had prepared for me to be a part of. When I entered her PT Cruiser, I was overtaken by the aroma of the best smelling fried chicken ever.

I wanted to dive straight into that box, but I didn't want to appear to be that overexcited by a box of chicken, so I fought off the temptation. When we made it to her home, I found it to be well kept and very homely. Time seemed to pass by so fast, and before I knew it we were headed to the halfway house. During that short visit, I really enjoyed her company. She then handed me a small bag with a cell phone inside. My first cell phone. It was a simple flip phone, but that meant nothing to me. She told me that was the only type of cell phones allowed at the halfway house, which was totally fine with me.

There was another bag with a few other personal items as well. I could recall a conversation she had with my mother, assuring her that I would be taken very good care of when I arrive in Colorado. I have to admit she hadn't missed a beat. And I mean from the very beginning of our loving relationship. She's been one of my most greatest blessings, and I couldn't wait to spend the rest of my life with her. When I made it to the halfway house, I thanked her for everything and gave her a big kiss. She drove away with a big smile. I then checked in, and I was given my room number.

I was placed with three other guys, and they were all friendly. At that moment, I felt totally free. Of course there were rules which I had no problem following. At the halfway house, they supplied the food, but we had to cook for ourselves. The room was really a one bedroom, with two small beds in the living room and two small beds in the bedroom. Of course, my bed was located in the living room. It had a full kitchen, one bathroom, a dining area, and plenty of food.

Once I got settled in, I couldn't wait to try out my first cell phone. I must have tried to call everyone I could think of because I didn't put that phone down until the wee hours the next morning. There was no greater joy than to be able to dial my mother's number whenever I felt like it and believe me, she enjoyed every call I made to her. My siblings and kids also shared that same degree of enjoyment with every call they received. Every moment there after was like endless moments of happiness. I couldn't have imagined this degree of happiness after so many years of sadness. My phone had limited features, but the one feature I enjoyed the most was the Facebook feature that I quickly learned everything about. Facebook allowed me the opportunity to reach out to all my loved ones and friends that I hadn't been in touch with for the last twenty-one years. It allowed me a way to not only say I'm back, but to show the world that of my physical presence as well. It also gave others the opportunity to reach out to me.

With so much free time on my hands, I stayed on Facebook. Matter of fact, Facebook brought about one of my greatest blessing since being set free. One day, I received this friend request, which I had received many since becoming a Facebook member. Without any hesitation, I would accept any and all friend request that came my way, whether I knew of them or not. So of course, I accepted this particular one. Later on in that day. I received a message that was thanking me for accepting their friend request. She then began to share this story with me concerning her own life.

She went on to say that when she was a baby, she was placed up for adoption, and that it wasn't until recently that she found out who her biological mother was. When she gave me her mother's name, a bell went off in my head, and I asked myself could this lady be the same young lady I used to date way back when? She went on to say that when she asked her mother who her father was, she told her my name. At that moment I was totally shocked. At the same time. I remembered her mother and I remembered the time I went to visit this little baby and yes, at that time her mother told me she was my child.

I knew there was a good possibility of her being mine, so I never denied that fact. When I tried to come back to visit her a week or so later, she was no place to be found. I later found out that she was seeing this other guy and didn't want to see me. So I simply left well enough alone and that was the last time I ever heard anything about her or the baby girl, until today. We talked for hours and that fatherly and daughterly bond connected automatically.

There wasn't a single doubt about her being my daughter, and I've loved her as if she's been a part of my life forever.

She informed me of all of my grandkids and they now all call me granddad. It will take her to tell you all, just how thankful and happy she is today with her daddy in her life, after so many years without knowing just who was responsible for giving her life. I can't thank God enough, not only for the blessing of freedom, but also for giving me and my daughter a clear path to one another's heart. I didn't hesitate sharing my newly found love with the world. My mother accepted her without question, as did her siblings, her uncles and aunts. She remains a permanent fix in all of our hearts. As I continued my journey into the light, I do so as humbly and gratefully as I can be.

CHAPTER 50

Life after Life

Nothing could have prepared me for life after life. What I thought I knew, I didn't have a clue. What I thought I was prepared for I simply wasn't. You would think that would be a problem, but I see it as a challenge that came with many opportunities. In my heart and soul, I had received the greatest blessing ever when I was granted clemency. Yet I had no idea of the full effects of that blessing. I had no idea that I became a part of history when I was granted clemency. I definitely didn't think I would be getting any type of media attention. But out of nowhere, I was contacted by this reporter from the *Denver Post*, and she informed me that they were interested in doing a full story on me. After two months and one day, I was now on my way out of the halfway house. It was April 17, 2014, the day my life started all over again. Not only was my fiancée outside waiting, so was the *Denver Post* reporter and her cameraman.

As I walked through that gate that stood between me and freedom, I did so as humbly as I could. The cameraman quickly snapped my picture, which I was sure he caught me looking down. I quickly made my way down to my fiancée and gave her the biggest hug. From that moment on, my life changed forever. And every step I took appeared to be in light speed. The *Denver Post* reporter in one car and my fiancée in the other, both with different agendas and forms of strategies. The *Denver Post* reporter placing all of her focus on the story at hand, which she entitled "A Lifetime Later. A Second Chance." My fiancée placing all of her focus on our wedding day that was only two days away. Just hours before I walked out of that halfway house entrance, me and my wife, her daughters and friends, went to Denver Office of the Clerk and Records to obtain our marriage license.

So much to do with only a short time to do it all. Hey, one would think this would be a lot on a man that been away for so many years, yet with every step I took it was like a dream coming true. I felt no pressure at all, even though with every step came things I knew not of until then. Life after life would take some time to get used to. I had very little time to think, for the most part I was being guided. For the two days leading up to my wedding day, I was being followed by *Denver Post*. *Denver Post* went as far as taking pictures of me catching the bus and joining me on my bus ride. The people on the bus didn't know what to think, but I felt like some kind of celebrity. I have to admit that all of this attention made me feel so special. At the same time, I didn't realize the magnitude of this whole ordeal.

Denver Post was with me when I took my first swim, when I got my first haircut as a free man, when I tried on my wedding attire, even when we went to get our wedding license, all the way up to the wedding itself as well as to the wedding reception, they were right there by my side.

With so many things happening all at once, there was virtually no time to relax. If I wasn't on the go, I was learning about something I didn't know about. Everything about the life I knew back then, had very little to do with the life I'm living today. I felt like a kid in a candy store for the very first time, but my candy store was truly the world itself. From seeing to tasting, from hearing to the mere presence of silence, from the words I was now free to utter at any given moment, everything brought me joy.

Sometimes I would overhear people complaining about how hard life is and what they don't have and what they think they may need, and I would say to myself if they had only walked in my shoes. God knows they would be singing a totally different tune, with a smile that matches that of my own. If I didn't learn nothing else within those twenty-one years of pain. I learned to appreciate a blessing of any size

To describe every detail leading up to our wedding day would truly take way too many more chapters, so I will attempt to simply outline the more intriguing moments leading up to our special day. From getting ready for our special day, to invitations, to family members flying in, to preparing for an Islamic wedding and a traditional wedding reception. We truly had no time to relax or get much sleep. My cousin Kim was the only family member from Texas able to make it, and when we picked her up from the airport, that was my first time seeing her in person since she was a very small child. Yet today she stood before me, a very beautiful young woman.

Her presence brought me so much joy, and I held her tightly within my arms. She arrived a day before my wedding day, and she stayed at our home the whole time she was here.

She had a college degree, and she was a certified beautician with her own beauty salon, in temple Texas called "Inspirational Styles." I'm so proud of her. My fiancée was also happy to meet my cousin. As a wedding gift, my cousin offered to do my wife's hair, which she accepted. Once she had finished, my wife's hair looked amazing. I have to admit; my lil cousin has some major skills when it comes to hair fashion.

In a nick of time, the day of our wedding, my fiancée's brother arrived, matter of fact. I had just gotten back from running a few errands, when I walked through the door and found him there. He informed me that my fiancée's and everyone had gone to the store. Being that this was our first-time meeting, this gave us the chance to formally introduce ourselves. Of course, being the big brother he was, he wanted to make sure that I truly had his little sister's best interest at heart.

After some straightforward question, I felt that my answers were sufficient and just as straightforward. I gathered by his demeanor thereafter. I met that of his approval. I had been forewarned by my fiancée that of his protective nature when it came to her, after all it was basely just the two of them growing up together. I will admit that he had that sternness about himself, which could have easily been viewed as a method of intimidation. Yet I see him as being just a big brother with genuine concern for his sister's well-being.

We were only a few hours away from our Islamic matrimony, and my phone wouldn't stop ringing. Everyone just wanted to know how things were coming along, especially my mother. Even though she was unable to make it down here, she still remained my top supporter. A title she's held down since the day I born. There's no way I could have made it to this day without her. She was one lady that stood against all odds when it came to her baby boy. There's truly no comparison to the love and devotion of a mother. The Islamic matrimony was short and sweet, as well as very heart touching. *The Denver Post* reporter was right there taking notes of this event as well as pictures. All I could do was praise God for all he has done. My heart was filled with joy and happiness as we made our way to the car. With time moving in rapid speed, we had little time to waste.

The traditional wedding reception awaited our arrival, with time working against us, we had no time to change out of our Islamic attire, so the plan was to do so after we got things ready at the reception hall. With our change of clothing with us, we made our way to the reception hall we had rented for the night. Everything went as planned and the wedding reception started on time, and the guests began to pour in.

To my surprise, my uncle and his wife were able to make it, which brought me so much joy. That made me have three of my family members there to represent my side of the family. Of course, *The Denver Post* reporter and cameraman were the first to arrive. They stayed for the first part of the reception. I wore a black suit with a gray vest and white shirt and a gray tie. I had no idea what my wife would be wearing until she appeared out of nowhere wearing this gray wedding gown and veil; she looked absolutely beautiful and with every step she made toward me, my heart melted.

I had to fight the tears away as she made her way into my arms. As we made our way to the middle of the dance floor as instructed by the DJ with the array of applause joining us, we enjoyed the first dance as Mr. and Mrs. Billy and Berna Wheelock, to the tune of Etta James song entitled "At Last." I could feel my Wife's heart racing, and I'm sure she could feel mine as we stepped to the beat of every tune. After our first dance, everyone else took the floor, and my wife was taken away as well by her brother as they danced into the night. This gave me some time to spend with my uncle and aunty. The cake cutting with congratulation speeches came thereafter. Tonight was filled with dreams coming true, with lives being changed, with faith being fulfilled, and with true love being lived. What more could I have wished for?

CHAPTER 51

Life after Life: The Conclusion

I've never been one that believed in fairy tale ending, yet on this very night no other words could describe this moment of my existence. From a condemned soul, that had no reason to believe, to the soul that never lost its faith. Even when the deepest of darkness consumed every illusion of light, faith continued to lead the way. As I stood outside the reception hall with a smile from ear to ear, words could not describe the pure happiness coming from my heart. This was truly one of my greatest moments in life. I made my way back inside to find my beautiful wife waiting for my return. We danced, we mingled, we laughed, while time passed us by. The day was and the night is everything we hoped it to be. Yet for me it was even more than I could have ever wished for. Everyone there shared our happiness. One of my wife's good friend who happened to be a well-known law professor at Denver University was so emotionally overtaken that he could no longer hold back the tears of happiness.

The professor is a great man that has very little faith in the justice system. He views the justice system as the ultimate bully who have for centuries overexerted its authority. The professor is also a man that don't bite his tongue, and he had no problem calling a spade a spade. He also taught his students those facts, with facts. As the night ended, the birth of a new life started. A life I couldn't begin to predict. *Denver Post* had completed their story on me and had informed me that it would be featured within a week or so. Sure enough, several days later on April 27, 2014, a day after my birthday, my story was featured on the front page of the *Denver Post*. The story would later be voted story of the year, which I found to be so rewarding on so many different levels. So far life after life has been filled with so many unbelievable moments, and I can't see anything other than many more unbelievable moments to come.

God himself is leading the way, and I'm following his every step. With the good, there is always a moment of sadness, a moment when God calls one of us home to him. On the twenty-sixth of April, on my birthday, my aunty was called home, and all I could think about was the many moments I spent in her presence. Her heart was always filled with joy and her love was visible to all. Even though I hadn't heard or seen her in over twenty-one years, the memories of her presence never left my heart.

I wasn't able to tell her I'm back and how much I've missed her and love her. But hopefully I'll be able to look upon her beauty one last time and say my goodbye. I'm not sure if that will be possible, but that won't stop me from trying. My wife had notice my sad mood and she decided to kick me out the house. Yes, and I mean literally, even though she knew how I felt about being out alone.

Of course I didn't agree with her choice of words and her actions, but being the man I was, I wasn't going to show her any fear.

So off I went, I had a checkup scheduled in a few days, so I thought I would find out how to get there, just in case. I found my way to the nearest bus stop and jumped on the first thing smoking. I got off near this shopping plaza, and just walked around and did a little window shopping. After a few hours went by, I got hungry and made my way to Wendy's. After being away for so many years, I was looking forward to the fast food life. I really enjoyed my day out and was looking forward to doing it again soon. I had to agree with my wife that the best way to learn my way around was to get out there. So that I did. Everything was so new to me and the outside movement around me was fast. So keeping pace was a challenge. I'm telling you, there were even times when I got lost.

In my own mind, I thought I was as normal as the next person, but I would soon learn I was so far from being normal. I can recall passing what appeared to be some sort of store from a distance. I never got a close view of that store, I always saw it from my bus stop which happened to be from a long distance. On this particular day, it started to rain at that bus stop, in fear that it would get worse, I decided to make way to the nearest building which happened to be that store I had never went to. When I made my way inside, sure enough it was a store, so I decided to see what they had at least until it stop raining.

So I grabbed a handbasket and started my shopping. I only had twenty dollars, so I knew I wouldn't be buying much. They had everything in this store. The first thing I saw was this giant bottle of strawberry soda, so I grabbed it. At the same time, I didn't see a price on the bottle, so I found the nearest employee their and asked her how much was this drink, she told me one dollar. I thanked her and went on my way. I was very happy about the sale price and was hoping that there would be more things here on sale.

The next thing that caught my eye was this big box of cereal, again I couldn't find a price on the box, so again I went to find the nearest employee, which happened to be the same young lady. Again I asked her the price of this item, this time she frowned and told me a dollar. I said to myself, *Hell if she had a price on these items I wouldn't have to ask her.* Anyway, I wasn't going to let her attitude ruin my sale day. I thought everything must be on sale. I needed me some triple A batteries, and found this eight pack, and again I couldn't find a price on that pack.

It had to be my luck, that same lady employer was the first person I saw and I didn't have a problem asking her again, this time she got a little loud and said, "Mister, everything in here is a *dollar.*" My eyes bucked wide open and I told her "Girl, that can't be true." And I ran off and grabbed this big bottle of cologne I've been looking at that I knew cost way too much and ran back to her and said, "I bet you this isn't a dollar." She said, "So sorry to inform you but yes that too is a dollar, just like everything else in here." She said with the biggest smile. I said, "Oh my god, I need me a basket."

I stayed in that store for an hour or more, until I had spent every penny of that twenty dollars. I couldn't wait to tell my wife or not. Because there were so many things even for her in there, so I thought about keeping it my secret. I thought about all the grandbabies I now have, and I could see myself taking them to my secret store and they asking me granddaddy can I have this or that and me saying, babies, get whatever you want, and how many you want. I was hoping my wife would be in our room, so I could sneak my bags inside. Sure enough she was inside our bedroom lying down.

I wasn't going to tell her but she is my wife and she deserved to know. So I told her in a whisper. I didn't know why I was whispering, but anyway, I told her about this store I found, and how we could buy gifts for everyone for the low low. I said, "Baby, *everything* in there is a dollar." She quickly said "Billy, you've been to the Dollar Tree." I said, "Girl, you know about that store?" She said, "Billy *everybody* knows about the Dollar Tree." I said yeah, and yes my bubble was busted, but I had to say it. I don't care, that's *still* my favorite store.

Life after life is constantly reminding me just how far I must go to truly fit back into society. I must crawl before I walk or I will never regain full capacity of self. So I have to take my time and allow life to meet me halfway. Very few can truly understand the full effects that comes with being confined in a place like prison for more than twenty years. Even a person that lived under those conditions has a problem understanding. I mean how could one understand something that himself doesn't know exist. The person you were, isn't the person you've grown to be within those twenty years, and that person you've grown to be has no clue to what he will be as a free individual. Yet freedom gives you back the chance to rewrite your wrongs, and to live out your God-given abilities. Every story has its own ending, and all we can do is to do our very best, to make our ending as good as it can be.

Today is a good day because today I have made plan to go visit my family, and to attend my aunt's funeral. I'm planning on a surprise visit, but I will have to let my big sister and my cousin know because they will be the ones to pick me up from the airport. No one else will know including my mother. This will also be my first airplane ride without being totally handcuffed. I'm so excited about seeing my mother, as well as my kids and all my family and friends. It's been over twenty-one years since I've been back home or seen my family members. I can't begin to share my true feelings concerning this trip back home to Texas. With such short notice, my wife will not be able to join me, but she's very excited about me going home after so many years away. The thought of seeing my mother as a free man brings nothing but joy to my heart. Yes, we talk over the phone every day, but that's nothing like seeing her beauty face to face. I truly owe my mother the world because she never left my side and her faith stayed rock solid.

This day couldn't have gotten here any faster. My first trip home, and I'm only a couple of hours away. My aunt from here is joining on my plane ride because she's on her way to the funeral as well. We should be arriving in Texas in the early part of the evening. It's now close to Thursday the noon hour, and we are about to board the plane. I'm so excited I can't even think straight. The plane ride was out of this world, and I decided right then and there that any long distance traveling I would always choose to fly. I even choose the window seat. It was truly a very enjoyable flight for me and my aunt. When we arrived in Texas, my first cousin picked us up. I hadn't seen her in years, and it felt like a lifetime had went by. We just held on tightly to one another, and it was like not a day had passed us by after our embracement.

She now lived in Dallas, and that's were our plane ride ended. So the plan was for her to pick us up and take us to meet my big sister and cousin half way. The Dallas airport was 120 miles from my hometown. So we had to drive sixty miles to meet them. When we arrived, my big sister rushed out of the car and ran up and gave me the biggest hug ever, and tears of joy followed, she couldn't hold them back and I could feel every weight of my twenty-one years' absence in her life leave her body. As I looked upon her beauty, the first thing I saw was my mother being reborn through her daughter. I didn't have to wait sixty more miles to see my mother's presence, for she stood before me as a reminder that she shall always be there for us through the fruits of her loins. We said our goodbyes to our first cousin and started on our way.

Within an hour or so, we had made it to my home-town. We had to take my aunt to my stepmother's house first, which I haven't seen in years, and she's always been like a second mother so I was looking forward to seeing her as well. I also was looking forward to seeing the place my father spent his last days and nights. When I arrive there, everywhere you turned I could feel his presence and there was many pictures of my father, after greeting my step-mother with a big hug and a kiss of the cheek. I found my way to one of my father's most resent pictures, and I let him know how much I loved him and just how much he's being missed and then I said my goodbyes, and I let him know that I would be making him proud of the man I've become.

Finally, I was on my way to see the world of my heart. Now remember no one knew I was coming. So when we got to my mother's house. I had my big sister and cousin to go inside first. To our surprise, my mother had company, it was one of her best friends that had come over. Nevertheless, the surprise must go on, once my sister and cousin walked in, out of nowhere I strolled in with my latest dance moves, just grooving with the pure happiness of this moment, my mother just sat there with this look that almost brought tears to my eyes, and even though the room had light, my mother instructed her boyfriend, Jeremiah, to turn on more lights.

She then screamed out, "Look at my baby!" as tears of joy fell softly upon her cheeks. I danced my way into her arms, and at that moment I was no longer this fifty-one-year-old man standing. No. I was that infant in the strong arms of his mother, and I had no concerns or fears, for I now laid in the arms of my guardian, my provider, my supporter, my protector, my mother. God hasn't given me the words to truly describe this very moment, and if I tried to do so, surely it would take the time of writing that of another book.

Within minutes, my mother's home was filled with my brother and his fiancée, more cousins, and my youngest daughter which happened to be the last child of mine I saw more than twenty-one years ago. She was only a baby sitting on the other side of a jail visitation window. Now she stands before me, a grown woman with three kids of her own. As I held her in my arms for the very first time, I felt my baby, my little girl, my teenager, now my young lady. I felt the pains of my absence, as well as the joy of my presence. She proudly called me daddy, and I humbly called her my baby. To me, it felt like a family reunion. If I could have measured the joy in my mother's home that night, surely it would have reached the stars above.

I stayed up almost the whole night with my mother just talking about everything. The next morning, I made my rounds and I saw all my children, my boys were now men. They were so happy to see their father, and I was even more happy to see them. The next day we put my aunt to rest, and I saw even more of my loved ones and friends. I spent time with my two brothers, and all my sisters, and we had a blast. Before I knew it, I was on my way back to Denver, filled with a love like no other. All I could do was thank God for allowing me to see my mother, and the rest of my family and friends. When I got back, my wife welcomed me with wide open arms.

A few weeks later, we are on our way to Washington, D.C. on a three-day fully paid trip to meet with some of the Congress members. Something I had only dreamed of doing, yet today I was on my way to do just that. I wrote of such a meeting when I was still in prison, now I'm blessed with the opportunity to live out that dream. It wouldn't stop there, interview after interview, speaking engagement after speaking engagement. I will forever be known as one of the Obama Eight. Not only that, you can now google my name and read about my whole twenty-one year journey. Life after life took on its own meaning in my life and the doors continue to open. From a life sentence. I, Billy Ray Wheelock, now share a part of history.

This is my story, now I'm waiting to read yours.

The End

Billy Ray Wheelock is one of the **"Obama Eight,"** a group of former prisoners who were all convicted of drug crimes and among the first to have their sentences commuted by President Obama.

THE OBAMA EIGHT

AS SEEN ON

THE WHITE HOUSE
WASHINGTON

USA TODAY

BuzzFeed

THE HUFFINGTON POST

10NEWS
TAMPA BAY SARASOTA
WTSP.COM · TEGNA

Los Angeles Times

The Dallas Morning News

THE DENVER POST

The Washington Times

CLARION

UNIVERSITY of DENVER

BILLY RAY WHEELOCK

is one of the Obama 8 that was granted clemency based on his drug crime. Billy's sentence was handed down by a Texas court in 1993, during the heyday of the war on drugs.

Crack was perceived as more addictive and dangerous then, and sentences for crack-related offenses were sometimes 100 times greater than for crimes involving the same amount of powder cocaine.

Billy was convicted and given Life in prison for selling 99.64 grams (little more than 3 ounces) of crack cocaine. On Dec. 19, in a clemency order that acknowledged *"a disparity in the law that is now recognized as unjust,"* President Barack Obama shortened the sentences of Wheelock and seven other men and women serving long prison terms for cocaine-related crimes, and Billy walked free after serving 21 years of a life sentence.

FAITHWITHOUTADATE

MAKINGHEADLINES

President Obama Grants Pardons and Commutation
The Whitehouse ◊ Dec 19, 2013

The Thoughts of a Pardoned Man - Billy Ray Wheelock
Cannabis Cheri ◊ Dec 23, 2013

A Hero among Nonviolent Drug Offenders
The New York Times Jan 26, 2014

Granted clemency, Billy Wheelock begins new life after prison
The Denver Post ◊ Apr 27, 2014

Granted clemency, man begins new life after prison
The Washington Times ◊ Apr 27, 2014

Meet the Former Crack Dealer Who Wants To Teach Congress about Drug Laws
BuzzFeed ◊ May 20, 2014

He's no longer a prisoner of the war on drugs
Los Angeles Times ◊ Sep 26, 2014

A second chance for Billy Ray Wheelock
USA Today ◊ Jul 29, 2015

CURRENTPROJECTS in development....

NEW BOOK COMING SOON!

FAITH WITHOUT A DATE, LLC
NON PROFIT

FAITH WITHOUT A DATE is a memoir of my life and legal experiences that happened behind the LIFE sentence and how I endured the long fight for freedom

MISSION to use my life story and experience as an **ADVOCATE** to change laws for **sensible sentencing** reform through the transference of existing resources from unnecessary incarceration **to proven programs** to reduce **recidivism**, and develop programs for lives harmed by unfair prison sentences to work constructively for change in their life, improving our society.

SPEAKING & INTERVIEW TOPICS

Mandatory Minimum Sentencing - The New Class of Modern Day Slavery
Sensible Sentence Reform, Shifting Resources in Punishment to Profit
Harsh Punishment – The REALISM of how Fact is turned into Fiction
Faith Without A Date – My Life, My Struggle, My Faith, My Freedom

CONTACT & CONNECT

Entheos Consulting Group manages all of **Billy Ray Wheelock's** interviews, press inquiries and informational requests from the media. The contact listed on this page are exclusively for media inquiries and speaking opportunities.

SOCIALMEDIA
About.me/billyraywheelock
Facebook www.facebook.com/pages/Billy-Ray-Wheelock
Twitter @seldomlyheard

For corporate, nonprofit, and general publicity inquiries for Mr. Billy Ray Wheelock,

227

This Former LIFER Says.....
Our Next Generation will be an America of Criminals

The United States has the largest prison population
in the world and the second-highest per-capita incarceration rate.

In 2013 in the USA, there were **698 people incarcerated per 100,000 population**.
According to the U.S. Bureau of Justice Statistics, **1 in 110 adults** were incarcerated in U.S. federal,
state prisons, and county jails in the US population in 2013, roughly about **2,220,300 adults**.
About **1 in 51 adults** are on probation or on parole in 2013, roughly about **4,751,400 adults**.
And **1 in 35 adults** are under correctional supervision in 2013, roughly about **6,899,000 adults**.

And that's **not** including the **54,148 juveniles** in juvenile detention in 2013.

According to a 2014 Human Rights Watch report,
"tough-on-crime" laws that were adopted in the 1980s
have filled U.S. prisons with mostly nonviolent offenders.
This policy failed to rehabilitate prisoners and many
were worse on release than before incarceration.

**Rehabilitation programs for offenders
can be more cost effective than prison.**

An energetic speaker who can address a **diversity of crime and
sentencing reform related issues**, **Billy Ray Wheelock** is one of
the **Obama 8** that was granted clemency based on his drug crime.
Billy's sentence was handed down by a Texas court in 1993, during the
heyday of the war on drugs. Billy was convicted and given LIFE in prison
for selling 99.64 grams (little more than 3 ounces) of crack cocaine.

On Dec. 19, in a clemency order that acknowledged *"a disparity in the law
that is now recognized as unjust,"* President Barack Obama shortened the
sentences of Wheelock and seven other men and women serving long
prison terms for cocaine-related crimes, and Billy walked free after serving
21 years of a life sentence.

Billy will keep your audience engaged and will bring home issues
that are not being addressed in current politics or in the justice system
such as:

Mandatory Minimum Sentencing - The New Class of Modern Day Slavery
Sensible Sentence Reform - Shifting Resources in Punishment to Profit
Harsh Punishment - The REALISM of how Fact is turned into Fiction
Faith Without A Date - My Life, My Struggle, My Faith, My Freedom

Billy Ray Wheelock is one of the **"Obama Eight,"**
a group of former prisoners who were all convicted
of drug crimes and among the first to have their
sentences commuted by President Obama.

AS SEEN ON

THE WHITE HOUSE
WASHINGTON

The Washington Times

THE
HUFFINGTON
POST

USA
TODAY

UNIVERSITY of
DENVER

Los Angeles Times

BuzzFeed

THE DENVER POST

CPSIA information can be obtained
at www.ICGtesting.com
Printed in the USA
LVHW092016290419
616025LV00006B/28/P

9 781640 966116